Green **Line**

4

von
Marion Horner
Pauline Ashworth
Jennifer Baer-Enge
Elizabeth Daymond
Paul Dennis

herausgegeben von
Harald Weisshaar

Ernst Klett Verlag
Stuttgart · Leipzig

Green Line 4   Workbook
für Klasse 8 an Gymnasien und für den Bildungsstandard Klasse 8 in Baden-Württemberg

Herausgeber: Harald Weisshaar, Bisingen
unter besonderer Mitwirkung von Frank Haß, Kirchberg

Autoren: Marion Horner M.A., Cambridge; Pauline Ashworth, Stuttgart; Jennifer Baer-Engel, Göppingen;
Elizabeth Daymond M.A., Kiel; Paul Dennis M.A., Lahnstein sowie Peter Lampater, Ehingen; Elin Arbin M.A., Freiburg

Berater: Jörg Nieswand, Berlin

Zeichenerklärung:

- ◎ Diese Texte und Übungen sind auf den Schüler- und auf den Lehrer-CDs.
- 👥 Diese Übungen / Übungsteile sind Partnerarbeit.
- 👥👥 Diese Übungen / Übungsteile sind Gruppenarbeit.
- Diese Übungen / Übungsteile sind besonders knifflig oder anspruchsvoll.
- Diese Übungen / Übungsteile sind besonders leicht.

1. Auflage   16 15
                   1 | 2020 19

Alle Drucke dieser Auflage sind unverändert und können im Unterricht nebeneinander verwendet werden.
Die letzte Zahl bezeichnet das Jahr des Druckes.

Redaktion: Susanne Vetter
Herstellung: Anita Bauch

Gestaltung: Anita Bauch
Umschlaggestaltung: Koma Amok, Stuttgart
Illustrationen: Lars Benecke, Hannover; Naomi Fearn, Berlin *(Kelsey)*
Satz: Wiebke Hengst, Ostfildern
Reproduktion: Meyle + Müller, Medien-Management, Pforzheim
Druck: Gebr. Geiselberger GmbH, Altötting

Printed in Germany
ISBN 978-3-12-547155-0 (Workbook mit Audio-CDs)
ISBN 978-3-12-547158-1 (Workbook mit Audio-CDs und Lernsoftware)

Audio-CD
Aufnahmeleitung: Ernst Klett Verlag GmbH, Stuttgart
Redaktion: Dr. Gregory Fuller
Produktion: Andrew Branch, RBA Productions, Brighton
Sprecherinnen und Sprecher: Jenny Bryce, Jason Durran, DeNica Fairman, Elly Fairman, Amy Finnegan, James Goode, Garrick Hagon, Laurel Lefkow, Walter Lewis, Allen Lidkey, Naomi McDonald, David Menkin, Eric Meyers, Alanis Peart, Nigel Pilkington, Christopher Ragland, Julie Rogers, Liza Ross, Martin T. Sherman, Amy Shindler, Adam Sims, Becca Stewart, Greg Wohead, Jennifer Woodward, Jo Wyatt
Aufnahme: The Audio Workshop, London
Tontechnik: Joseph Degnan
Presswerk: P+O Compact Disc GmbH & Co.KG, Diepholz

Gesamtzeit: CD 1 – 51'13"; CD 2 – 74'14"

Hi there!
Willkommen im Workbook!
Bevor es losgeht, erkläre
ich dir kurz, was dich
erwartet.

- Wie im Schülerbuch sind auch im Workbook die Units 1, 3 und 5 Langunits und die Units 2 und 4 Kurzunits.
- In den Kurzunits hast du die Wahl zwischen Text A und Text B. Du darfst natürlich auch beide Seiten bearbeiten.
- Außerdem gibt es in den Kurzunits wie im Schülerbuch eine Seite zu *Writing texts*. In den Langunits gibt es zusätzlich noch eine Übung zu *Writing texts*, die dir hilft, deine Schreibfertigkeiten zu verbessern.
- Nach Unit 2 und 5 kannst du auf zusätzlichen *Revision*-Seiten überprüfen, ob du den neuen Stoff richtig verstanden hast.
- Wie im Schülerbuch gibt es auch im Workbook drei spannende Geschichten mit interessanten und kniffligen Aufgaben.
- Auf der *Skills*-Seiten in jeder Unit findest du nützliche Tipps zum Hören, Sprechen, Grammatik usw.
- Zusätzlich zu den *Skills*-Seiten in jeder Unit findest du auf den Seiten 74–78 weitere *Skills*. Hier übst du noch einmal intensiv *Group-*, *Writing-*, *Speaking-*, *Vocabulary-* und *Reading-Skills*. Die wichtigsten Tipps zu den einzelnen *Skills* sind darin übersichtlich zusammengefasst.

Noch ein paar Worte zur Arbeitsweise mit dem Workbook: Dein Lehrer/deine Lehrerin korrigiert deine Arbeit im Workbook oder ihr besprecht die Übungen gemeinsam im Unterricht.
Die Übungen auf den *Check-out*-Seiten kannst du jedoch selber korrigieren! Die Lösungen zum

Überprüfen deiner Ergebnisse findest du am Ende des Workbooks.
So, das war's. Dann kann die Reise durch die USA losgehen!

Viel Spaß und Erfolg mit **Green Line 4**!

Unit 1 New York City

1 Put in the correct words and names (→ PB p. 12)

A German boy in New York is e-mailing some photos to a friend in the UK. Complete what he writes.

1. This is the ___Empire___ State _____ . Sorry, my photo doesn't show all of the 102 _____ ! It was great to stand at the top of one of the world's tallest _____ . An _____ shot me up there in less than a minute!

2. Lots of people from the other four _____ of New York City come to work in Manhattan. Every day four and a half _____ passengers travel on the _____ . I think they were all on the _____ I took this photo in!

3. I didn't want to look into the windows of all the _____ on Fifth _____ with my mother. So while she went there, I went to _____ Park, not far away from there. I had a great time with these kids I _____ there.

4. The _____ of Liberty says hello to you, too! Like more than one in three of the _____ million New _____ she was born outside the _____ States. She came here from France. Well, she doesn't really look very French, does she?

2 Listening: Tips for tourists (→ PB p. 12)

a) *Read the questions and listen for the information. Write your answers in note form.*

1. Which country gave the Statue of Liberty to the US? – _____

2. Which way do avenues run? – _____

3. What do bus drivers not do? – _____

4. Where can you buy Metrocards? – _____

b) *Now listen for these numbers and dates and explain what information the guide gives. Use your exercise book.*

   10   1886   13   1907

3 Make present perfect progressive forms (→ PB p. 14; Grammar → PB G1)

The people who work in this diner have been busy with the same jobs all morning.
Use the verbs in the picture and write down what they have been doing.

1. __She has been making coffee.__

2. __They__

3. __He__

4. _____

5. _____

6. _____

4 Put the words and phrases with the correct preposition (→ PB p. 14; Grammar → PB G2)

a year ✔ • an hour • last year ✔ • 6 o'clock • a long time • my birthday • I arrived • I was 6 • two days

since	for
last year,	a year,

5 Complete these New York 'cab' dialogues (→ PB p. 15; Grammar → PB G2)

Put in present perfect progressive forms and for or since.
Use the verbs on the right.

drive
worry   rain   make
try ✔
do

1. Passenger: I __'ve been trying__ to get a cab _____ the rain started.

   Cab driver: Wow, you had to wait a long time! It _____ _____ ten minutes.

2. Cab driver: Sorry, but my cab _____ a strange noise _____ this morning.

   Passenger: Yes, I _____ about it _____ I got in. I hope we get to the hotel in one piece!

3. Passenger: We _____ around _____ a long time. Are you sure you know the way?

   Cab driver: I _____ this job _____ twenty years. So yes – I know the way!

6 **How to: Get someone's attention** (→ PB p. 15)

a) *It is easier to get someone's attention if you only use a few words. What short phrases would be better than these long sentences? The Useful phrases on page 15 of your book can help you.*

1. "Could I have coffee, please, and also eggs with toast and – oh dear, he still isn't listening to me."

   – _____

2. "Would you please come to this side so that I can take a good photo of you, too?"

   – _____

3. "You shouldn't try to buy your ticket before me when I've been waiting longer than you."

   – _____

4. "Please come back so that I can give you this – it's just fallen out of your pocket."

   – _____

b) *Prepare your own situation. Act it out.*

7 **Explain what the people had been doing** (→ PB p. 16; Grammar → PB G3)

Read why some New Yorkers were taken to the hospital yesterday. Then find the correct ideas to explain what they had been doing at the time and make sentences with past perfect progressive forms. Use your exercise book.

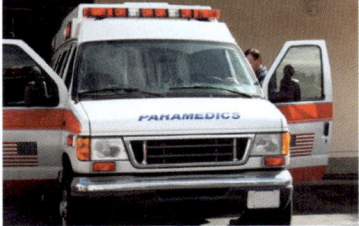

Example: 1. A young woman was taken to the hospital yesterday because she had hurt her back.
She had been putting heavy boxes into her car.

1. A young woman … (hurt) her back.
2. A man … (become) sick during a race.
3. A cook … (cut) his hand badly.
4. A little boy … (be hit) by a car.
5. A worker … (fall) from a building.
6. A dancer … (broke) her leg on stage.

- run after a ball
- perform in a new show
- prepare vegetables with a big knife
- put heavy boxes into her car
- mend a hole in the roof
- try too hard to win the race

8 **Complete what someone says about a trip to New York** (→ PB p. 16; Grammar → PB G3)

*Use the past perfect progressive with **for** or **since**.*

1. I was glad when I finally arrived at the airport. (sit on the plane / over six hours)

   <u>I had been sitting</u> _____.

2. It was great to meet my American friend for the first time. (write to her / two years)

   _____.

3. I already knew about some of the sights she showed me. (read brochures / the invitation arrived)

   _____.

4. My week in New York was everything I had hoped. (dream of a trip to New York / I was a child)

   _____.

9 Mediation: In a hotel

You and your family are staying in a small hotel in New York. You speak the best English, so you have to speak to the man there. Write down what you can say in the different situations. Use your exercise book.

1. „Frag' mal, ob er uns ein kleines Restaurant in der Nähe empfehlen kann."
2. „Sage, dass das Licht im Bad seit heute Morgen streikt. Ohne Licht müssen wir ja die Tür auflassen!"
3. „Wir wollen morgen früher aufstehen. Bitte ihn, uns um acht zu wecken."
4. „Frage ihn, ob er weiß, wo wir Geld umtauschen können."
5. „Hm, ob es auch Broschüren auf Deutsch gibt? Ich sehe nur welche auf Englisch und Französisch."
6. „Unser Flug geht erst am Abend. Frag' ihn bitte, ob es möglich ist, unser Gepäck bis zum späten Nachmittag irgendwo abzustellen, nachdem wir unsere Zimmer geräumt haben."

10 Team activity: Plan a day in Manhattan

a) *Get together in groups of four. Split up into pairs in your group. Look at the information you have from a guidebook. Discuss all the different ideas with your partner and plan a day in Manhattan that you will all enjoy. Follow these rules:*

- You cannot do everything in one day, so you are allowed to visit no more than four places.
- Together you must spend no more than $100. (Don't forget to leave a few dollars for lunch!)

b) *Now discuss your results in your group and agree on one plan for your group.*

A great way to see **Chinatown** is to go on a walking tour. Your guide will tell you all about the history and culture of one of the oldest parts of New York.
Tours start 10:30 am–5:00 pm and last 1½ hours. Price: $15.

You don't always have to pay to have a good time! **Central Park** is the green part of Manhattan. It's a great place to walk, skate or row a boat – or just to sit and relax between visits to some of the other sights.

The views from the top of the **Empire State Building** are fantastic, day or night. Open daily 8:00 am–2:00 am. Last elevators at 1:15 am.
Admission: Adults (over 18) $19, Youth (12–17) $17, Children (6–11) $13.

Take the chance to see where the rich buy their clothes! You can find almost every famous name in the world of high fashion on **Madison Avenue**. It's fun to go window-shopping there, and it doesn't cost anything to look!

The best way to see the famous Manhattan skyline is from the water. The 3-hour **Full Island Boat Tour** costs $29, (Children under 13: $16). There is also a 2-hour **Harbor Lights Evening Tour** ($24, Children $13).

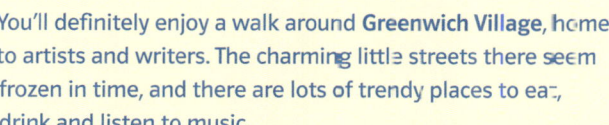

You'll definitely enjoy a walk around **Greenwich Village**, home to artists and writers. The charming little streets there seem frozen in time, and there are lots of trendy places to eat, drink and listen to music.

New York is one of the culture capitals of the world, so **MoMA** (the Museum of Modern Art) should definitely be on your list of places to go during your stay. Open 10:30 am–5:30 pm.
Prices: Adults $20, Children (16 and under) free.

One of the most important places in New York, and also in the world, is the **United Nations** building. Guided tours are offered daily. Prices: Adults $13, Students $9, Children (5–14 years old) $7.

TALKWISE

11   **Match the feelings to the pictures**   (→ PB p. 17)

angry • happy • scared • excited • surprised • sad

1 _____

2 _____

3 _____

4 _____

5 _____

6 _____

12   **Listening: Listen for the feeling the voice expresses**   (→ PB p. 17)

a) *Listen to the words, think what feeling the voice expresses and tick (✔) the right box.*

1. "Oh, tell me about it."	a) expectation	☐	b) sympathy	☐
2. "I have a hundred dollars."	a) surprise	☐	b) happiness	☐
3. "Lots of famous people will be there."	a) expectation	☐	b) surprise	☐
4. "This is what life is about."	a) sympathy	☐	b) happiness	☐

b) *Listen again. This time you will hear the words from a) with both feelings. After each person has spoken, stop and repeat the words yourself. Try to show the feeling with your voice.*

13   **Short dialogues**   (→ PB p. 17)

Match the correct four pairs of speakers. Write the dialogues down.
Then underline the phrases that express the main feeling in each dialogue, and write down what this feeling is. Use your exercise book.

"I was sick while I was away on vacation." • "I'm sure you are. It's a great feeling to fall in love!" • "I'm really looking forward to it, too." • "Suddenly I'm on top of the world." • "I have some good news for you. You got first prize." • "I'm sorry to hear that. That was bad luck." • "I can't wait to go to the concert tonight." • "Wow, that's amazing! I didn't expect to win."

14   **Write down what you would say in these situations**   (→ PB p. 17)

The Useful phrases on page 17 of your book will help you to express your feelings.
Use your exercise book.

1. A famous star was once a student at your school, and he is visiting the school next Friday.
2. You are listening to the news. A factory has closed and hundreds of people have lost their jobs.
3. It is a beautiful day and you are on a bike tour with your best friend.
4. It is your birthday and you have just found out that your friends have planned a party for you.

15 Finish the sentences with the correct words and adjectives   (→ PB p. 18; Grammar → PB G4)

| me • English • anyone • city • words • them | + | happy • exciting ✔ • clear • rich • asleep • difficult |

1. New York is a great place to be a tourist guide because everyone finds

   this __city exciting__ .

2. I really enjoy the work, although I don't earn a lot – so my job will never make _____ .

3. I find small groups better because it's easier to look after people and keep _____ .

4. I'm glad to say that on my tours I haven't often seen _____ .

5. Of course tourists who speak other languages sometimes find _____ .

6. So with groups like that I speak very carefully and try to make my _____ .

16 Revision: Adjectives or adverbs?   (→ PB p. 19)

TIP
Remember: Some verbs are followed by an adjective.

It is (interesting) _____ to watch people (careful) _____

in the (busy) _____ streets of Manhattan and to see how

(different) _____ they behave. Some tourists stay (calm)

_____ , while others run around (excited) _____ .

You can (easy) _____ see which people are New Yorkers. Many

of them wear (nice) _____ suits because for them it is a (normal)

_____ day at the office. Some New Yorkers earn very (good)

_____ , but they (regular) _____ have to work long

hours, so they like to get to work (fast) _____ !

17 Rewrite the speakers' words with the adverbs of degree   (→ PB p. 19; Grammar → PB G5, 6)

1. These pictures are awful. (pretty) __These pictures are pretty awful__ .

2. Oh, I have to say, I like them. (quite) __Oh, I have to say, I__ _____ .

3. This one is painted well. (extremely) _____ .

4. The man's head looks big. (too) _____ .

5. No, you're wrong about that. (completely) _____ .

18 How to: Say you liked it (→ PB p. 19)

*Make dialogues about great activities or places
in New York. Take turns to play A and B.
Use the Useful phrases on p. 19 in your book.*

Example: A: What was the Statue of Liberty like?
      B: It was really amazing. It seems even
          bigger when you stand next to it!

19 Revision: Use present perfect or simple past forms (→ PB p. 20)

*Find the correct ideas to complete the dialogue and put the verbs
into the present perfect or simple past.*

see your passport • never do anything silly • give it to you • not find it yet • just remember •
get here a week ago • lose your camera last year

A: I'm still looking for my passport. I _____ .

B: You always lose things on vacation. You _____ .

A: Oh, sorry. I'm not perfect like you! Of course, you _____ .

B: Come on, let's not have an argument. Try to remember the last time you_____ .

    I don't expect you've had to use it since we _____ .

A: That's right. I had to show it when we arrived, and then – Hey, _____ .

    You've got my passport. After you warned me not to lose it, I _____ !

20 Listening: The General Slocum[1] (→ PB p. 20)

Tick all the boxes with the correct information. (More than one answer may be correct.)

1. The trip on June 15, 1904 was organized by
    a) a club in Kleindeutschland. ☐
    b) a restaurant in the neighborhood. ☐
    c) a German church. ☐

2. The men who worked on the General Slocum
    a) were not trained for emergencies. ☐
    b) did not notice the fire at first. ☐
    c) only had old and broken equipment. ☐

3. The captain decided to go on because
    a) he was scared to stop in the East River. ☐
    b) there was a lot of oil next to the river. ☐
    c) there were too many other boats. ☐

4. Most of the 1021 people who lost their lives
    a) died in the fire on the ship. ☐
    b) jumped into the water and drowned. ☐
    c) were children. ☐

5. In the years after the fire on the General Slocum
    a) a statue was made to remember the dead. ☐
    b) a lot of German families moved away. ☐
    c) Kleindeutschland became East Village. ☐

[1]General Slocum [ˌdʒɛnrl ˈsləʊkəm]

LISTENING SKILLS

21 **Listen to American and British accents** (→ PB p. 21)

Listen to what some people in a restaurant say. Underline the words with the sounds that help you to recognize the speakers' nationality. Then write down whether they come from the US or the UK.

1. "Oh, good. The waiter is coming to our table at last." – _____

2. "Excuse me! Could I have a glass of water, please?" – _____

3. "This looks almost too beautiful to eat – it's like a work of art!" – _____

4. "I don't know what I should order because it all sounds so good." – _____

5. "I'm pretty sure the family at the next table is British." – _____

22 **Understand English that does not follow the rules** (→ PB p. 21)

There are a lot of colloquial forms, 'wrong' grammar and missing words in the text. Rewrite the dialogue in 'correct' English. Use your exercise book.

Lisa: Well, guys, what pictures are you gonna work into your mural?
Boy: We dunno yet. Ain't so easy to make a design when you ain't never done nothin' like it before.
Lisa: Well, what kinda themes you been thinkin' of? If you gimme some ideas, maybe I can help.
Girl: We wanna show somethin' from our own lives. Kids in this neighborhood have a whole lotta problems.
Boy: But the design's also gotta show there's ways you can deal with those problems. I mean, it don't help nobody to say there ain't no solution.

23 **Listen for keywords** (→ PB p. 21)

Listen to the three conversations and write down a few keywords to help you understand the gist of the text. Then match each speaker with the right picture and give the other person's answer.

TIP

Get ready for all kinds of accents and grammar. Not everyone speaks English as their first language.

A

B

C

1. Keywords: _____ → Picture ___

   Answer: _____
   _____

2. Keywords: _____ → Picture ___

   Answer: _____

3. Keywords: _____ → Picture ___

   Answer: _____

24 **Draw lines to the correct endings** (→ PB p. 24)

1. Cathia Moise was born in Haiti, but

2. Her father died soon after

3. Many of her relatives also live in New York, although

4. People in the area look after Cathia because

5. She is not like the kids in that neighborhood who

they respect the way she behaves.

she has spent most of her life in New York.

drop out of school and get into trouble.

most have moved away from Harlem.

the family had arrived in the US.

25 **Take Cathia's part in this interview** (→ PB p. 24)

a) *A young reporter from 'Radio rookies' is interviewing Cathia Moise. Use the text in your book to help you, and write down her answers in your exercise book. If you start an answer with 'Yes' or 'No', you should also give the reasons for that answer.*

1. Who do you live with in this apartment, Cathia?
2. Do you remember much about your life in Haiti?
3. And what about life here on West 144th Street? What's this neighborhood like?
4. Don't you feel scared when you walk around in the street?
5. How are you doing at Philip Randolph High School? What activities do you do?
6. Would you say there's a lot of pressure on you at this time in your life?
7. What do you want to do with your life after school and college?
8. Why did you choose that job?

b) *Act the interview out. When you are Cathia, try not to look at your answers from a).*

26 **Writing texts: Opinions** (→ PB p. 24)

Some kids are expressing opinions in an Internet chatroom.
Read what they say and then give your own opinion on the topic.
Try to use some of the phrases you collected in exercise 4 a) on page 24 in your book.

Jez: I think it must be really great to play sports professionally. In my opinion, it's a dream job. Personally, I'd love to be a basketball player.

Lil: I don't believe it´s a realistic dream. The way I see it, there's almost no chance to become a star. If you ask me, it's better to work hard at school and go to college.

Jez
Lil

You: |_____

_____

_____

_____

Double click a name for a private chat.

27 Recognize American English (→ PB p. 25)

a) *Underline all the words which show that the person who wrote this is American, not British.*

b) *Rewrite the text with British English words.*
   Use your exercise book.

One day I'll be a movie star. I'll live in a beautiful apartment downtown. And when I want to go out, I'll call a cab to take me to all the best stores and restaurants. I'll also fly to amazing places on vacation, and I won't have to wait in a long line at the airport. – But until somebody discovers me, I'll just go on with my job in the candy store and go to work on the subway every day and dream!

28 Put in the correct prepositions

Peer mediators help to stop fights __between__ students _____ Philip Randolph High School.

Although fights might seem more typical _____ boys than girls, girls sometimes need to

ask _____ help, too. _____ the time students go _____ peer mediators, small

arguments often have turned _____ big ones, but the students are helped _____ the peer

mediators to talk _____ their problems.

29 Find the missing words (→ PB p. 25)

Think what the link is between the words in the first pair. Then you can complete the second pair.

1. London – Londoner

   New York – __New Yorker__

2. at the back – in front of

   at the bottom – _____

3. store – customer

   cab – _____

4. safe – safety

   happy – _____

5. sweets – candy

   taxi – _____

6. British – pounds

   American – _____

7. phone – telephone

   celeb – _____

8. Germany – German

   China – _____

9. dance – dancer

   art – _____

30 Just for fun: Signs in cabs

Read the signs. Then add your own ideas for the two cabs.

31   **Do a quiz about New York**   (→ PB p. 26)

*Answer the questions without your book. All the information is somewhere in Unit 1
or on the map at the back of your book.*

1. How many boroughs are there in New York City? – _____

2. How many people live in New York City? – _____

3. What is special about the cabs in New York? – _____

4. What kind of sports do the New York Yankees play? – _____

5. Where is the immigration center? – _____

6. In what year did terrorists attack the World Trade Center? – _____

32   **Make sentences with the present perfect progressive**   (→ PB p. 26; Grammar → PB G1, 2)

Find the correct ideas and complete what Diego and his family say.

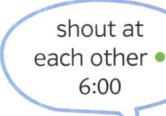 shout at each other • 6:00   cook • over twenty minutes   talk on the phone • ages   sit near the door • you got up

1. Diego: Elena! Other people want to call their friends, too, you know.

    You've been talking _____

2. Elena: It's your job to take the dog out this morning, Rob. Look, he's waiting.

    _____

3. Rob: I wish the people in the apartment above us would be quiet.

    _____

4. Wife: Hey, Diego! Who's the cook here? You forgot about the eggs!

    _____

33   **Describe the situation**   (→ PB p. 26; Grammar → PB G3)

*Suddenly yesterday evening there was no power in the Moises' apartment. Write down what they
had been doing before they had to stop. Look at what they say to find out. Find your own verbs.*

1. Maudeline: I was only on page 6! _She had been reading a book._ _____

2.   Wilfred: No power – no computer game! _He_ _____

3. Grandma: My favorite soap had just started. _____

4.   Cathia: I couldn't finish my project. _____

5. Grandad: Only half of the quiz is done! _____

34 What are they saying or thinking? (→ PB p. 27)

Look at the pictures and put the people's feelings into words.

1. _____

2. _____

3. _____

4. _____

35 Put the sentence parts in the right order (→ PB p. 27; Grammar → PB G5,6)

1. The New York subway …   very • in the morning • is • busy • usually

   The New York subway _____

2. Many thousands …   make • full • of passengers • extremely • the trains

   _____

3. Often …   enough • for everyone • there • seats • are not

   _____

4. A few people …   to get to a seat • push • first • in front of others • always

   _____

5. Other passengers …   selfish • find • the way • pretty • they behave

   _____

36 Use the correct word in the correct form: adjective or adverb (→ PB p. 27)

angry • quick • good • rude • patient • hard

Breakfast in Diego's Diner always tastes _____ . Diego also works _____ to try and give

you your food _____ . But he can't serve everyone right away, so sometimes you have to be

_____ . It isn't a good idea to make Diego _____ . When a customer shouted _____

at him yesterday, he threw the customer out!

〈American youth〉

Ted is 14 and lives in a New England town. He finds it hard to decide what is 'right' and 'wrong'. One afternoon, two friends from school come to his house. They are all terribly bored.

Although the Dennisons had air-conditioning and a swimming pool, the three boys were hot and bored that afternoon at the boy's home.

"You don't have crap[1] to do," Bobby said.

5 Bobby always said that there wasn't anything to do.

"He has a gun," Bobby's brother, Kevin, said.

"I don't believe it," Bobby laughed.

"He does."

10 "Show us," Bobby said.

"I have two," the boy told them.

"Let's see them," Bobby said.

"What kinds?" added Kevin.

"A twelve-gauge[2]," the boy told them. "And a
15 twenty-two[3]."

"Let's see the twelve-gauge," Kevin said.

The boy shook his head.

"He's scared," Bobby said. "That's why he won't."

20 The boy looked out the window and saw his mother working in the backyard. "I'll show you my twenty-two," he said.

"That's a stupid gun," Bobby said.

"Shut up," Kevin told his brother.

25 The boy shook his head. It wasn't stupid. His .22 was the only new gun in the house – his family had had the others for years: one under the couch in the living room, two in the garage, and one under his father's bed.

30 He took the brothers to the china cupboard in the living room. He reached[4] under it.

"Why here?" Kevin asked him.

"For the birds," he said.

Kevin looked confused[5].

35 "They wake my dad up some mornings," the boy said. "He lets me shoot them. Out the window." He glanced[6] over his shoulder at the window that looked out on the backyard.

"That's awesome," Kevin said.

40 The boy didn't say that he had never shot at anything yet. Every time he opened the window, the birds flew away. And he knew he couldn't shoot at them then – there were houses out there behind the woods[7], and a bullet[8] from a .22 could
45 go over a mile.

He took the gun out and held it gently.

He pointed the barrel[9] at the floor and told the Dennisons about the parts he knew. For a moment the brothers listened patiently.

"Let me hold it," Bobby said. 50

The boy pointed the barrel at the floor and gave him the gun. Bobby seemed surprised because it was so heavy. He smiled and pointed it at his brother.

"Bang," he said. "You're dead." 55

The boy took the gun away from him quickly.

"Never do that," he said.

"What?"

"Point it."

"It's not loaded[10]," Bobby said. "That's stupid." 60

"You're stupid," the boy said. He opened the cabinet[11] and took out a small box. "These are the bullets." He opened the box and took out one for them to see. The boy dropped it into Kevin's hand. The two brothers looked down at it. 65

"It's tiny," Bobby said.

"Show us how to put it in." Kevin gave the boy the bullet back.

The boy shook his head.

"Why not?" Bobby said, "We're inside." 70

"Come on," Kevin said. "Do it."

"Show us," Bobby said.

The boy looked at them. Their eyes seemed so excited. Kevin put the bullet in the boy's hand. He looked at Kevin and Bobby – then he showed 75 them. It felt beautiful the slide and click of steel on steel. He breathed out[12] and looked at them.

---

[1]**crap** [kræp] = *here:* anything • [2]**twelve gauge** ['twelv geɪdʒ] = name and size of a gun • [3]**twenty-two** [ˌtwenti'tuː] = name and size of a gun • [4]**to reach** [riːtʃ] = to put your hand • [5]**confused** [kən'fjuːzd] = not understanding anything • [6]**to glance at sth** ['glɑːns æt] = to look at sth for a short time • [7]**woods** [wʊdz] = area with lots of trees • [8]**bullet** ['bʊlɪt] = small round thing which is put in a gun • [9]**barrel** ['bærəl] = (Gewehr)Lauf • [10]**loaded** ['ləʊdɪd] = ready to shoot • [11]**cabinet** ['kæbɪnət] = cupboard • [12]**to breathe out** [briːð 'aʊt] = to let air out of nose / mouth

They smiled. Bobby moved from one foot to another.

80 The boy heard a noise outside and he walked to the window. His mother wasn't in the backyard. He looked nervously from the .22 to the Dennisons. He knew he would be in big trouble if he did what the boys wanted him to do.
85 He then put it back under the cabinet.

He moved quickly to the window in the other room and was glad to find her in the side yard. He felt guilty as he watched her work. He knew he should help her.

90 As he turned from the window, he suddenly heard the sound of the loud bang in the house. He was confused only for a moment. It was different inside, but he recognized the noise anyway. He started to shake. He was sure his
95 father would find out, would take his gun and get very angry and quiet for days. He wondered if he could hide the bullet hole.

As the boy got to the door of the room and saw Bobby on his back, he forgot that he was angry.
100 He felt like he couldn't breathe. He looked at Kevin. Kevin was crying.

"My ears," Kevin said.

"What?"

"My ears," he said. "I can't hear."

"What happened?" 105

"He wanted it and I was still looking at it. He pulled it." Kevin quickly gave the gun back to the boy and left the room. The boy walked toward Bobby. Blood came out of Bobby's mouth. His eyes opened and closed, but he didn't move 110 anything else. The boy moved closer and Bobby's eyes found him. He looked confused, like a dog when it heard a new sound. The boy almost jumped when Bobby moved. His hand came up and touched the small bloody spot[13] on his 115 chest[14]. Then his arm stopped and lay still again.

The boy looked down at the .22. He opened it and held out his hand to catch the rest of the bullet. He held it to his nose and smelled it. He put the gun back under the cabinet. He turned 120 and crouched[15], both feet under him, his elbows[16] on his knees. He watched Bobby carefully, the way he moved here and there. Bobby looked at the ceiling.

The boy turned when he heard a noise behind 125 him, and he was surprised to see his mother. He was scared of her punishment[17], but she didn't come for him. She didn't scream. She walked quickly over and fell to her knees next to Bobby.

"Call an ambulance," she said. 130

adapted from: *American Youth* by Phil LaMarche

---

[13] **spot** [spɒt] = Fleck • [14] **chest** [tʃest] = part of the body where the heart is • [15] **to crouch** [kraʊtʃ] = almost like sitting, but you are still on your feet • [16] **elbow** ['elbəʊ] = part of arm • [17] **punishment** ['pʌnɪʃmənt] = Strafe

---

1 Before you read

How do you think the boys will spend the afternoon? Collect ideas with a partner.

2 Work with the text

a) *Is there anything in the story that really surprised you? Why? Discuss with a partner.*

b) *Look at the adjectives in the text.*
Fill in the grid. Then find the nouns that belong to the adjectives.
Use the nouns and adjectives to make five sentences about the story.

positive adjectives / nouns	negative adjectives / nouns
small / box	_____
_____	_____
_____	_____
_____	_____
_____	_____

c) *Underline at least two parts in the story when Ted does things he does not really want to do. Why does he behave that way and what would have happened if he had behaved differently? Discuss with a partner.*

d) *Write a characterization[18] of Ted. Use your exercise book.*

e) *How do you expect the story to go on? Discuss with a partner. Do you think Bobby will die?*

---

[18] **characterization** [ˌkærəktraɪ'zeɪʃn] = Charakterisierung

〈Revision for tests〉 Unit 1

1 Understanding the text: The Big Apple

Why is New York City called the Big Apple?
The answer is: Nobody really knows. John J.
Fitzgerald[1] first used the name in the 1920s.
He wrote articles about horses and horse races
5 in New York for a New York newspaper. He met
some of the men from New Orleans[2] who looked
after the horses. They called New York the Big
Apple. To them the city seemed so big and gave
them so many chances to earn money. They
10 did not have chances like that where they came
from. He decided to call his article 'Around the
Big Apple'.
When, in the 1930s, and '40s, a jazz man said
he was playing at the Big Apple, everybody
15 knew he was talking about the best jazz club in
Manhattan – in Harlem.
So was it a jazz club or was it an article in a
newspaper that gave New York City its other
name? Or was it something else? In the 1930s

and '40s a group dance called the Big Apple 20
became popular in Harlem and around the US.
But soon people forgot the name Big Apple,
until in the 1970s an advertising agency[3] had
an idea when they were trying to think of ways
to get tourists to visit New York. They decided 25
to call the city the Big Apple to make it sound
interesting to tourists. The advertising agency
won a prize. Many people don't say Big Apple
anymore – but they come to visit New York City!

Complete the text.

_____ really knows exactly why _____ is called the _____ .

There are a lot of ideas. Maybe it is because people sold _____ on the streets in the

_____ . Some people think the name comes from a _____ in Harlem, or from

a _____ . In the 1920s there was also a newspaper _____ in a newspaper in

New York called 'Around the Big Apple'. One thing is sure, everybody would have forgotten the name if

an _____ had not used the Big Apple to advertise the city in _____ .

2 Listening: A really American game

Listen to this radio program about sports in the Big Apple.
Right, wrong or not in the text?

	right	wrong	not in the text
1. There are only professional baseball teams in the US.	☐	☐	☐
2. Baseball is a business and a kind of sports.	☐	☐	☐
3. The professional season is from April to September.	☐	☐	☐
4. The first team which wins four games is the champion.	☐	☐	☐
5. The Yankees became the world baseball champion in 2001.	☐	☐	☐
6. Japan and Cuba play baseball, too.	☐	☐	☐

[1]**Fitzgerald** [fɪts'dʒerəld] • [2]**New Orleans** [ˌnjuː ˈɔːrliənz] • [3]**advertising agency** [ˈædvətaɪzɪŋ ˌeɪdʒnsi] = Werbeagentur

3   **Writing texts: Joe Di Maggio[4]**

Use these notes to write a profile[5] about Joe Di Maggio for the sports page in your school magazine. Use your exercise book.

1914:	parents' immigration to US from Sicily[6]; born in Martinez[7], California; eighth of nine children
1915:	moved with family to San Francisco
1932:	joined baseball club 'San Francisco Seals[8]'
1934:	hurt left knee, but got better; New York Yankees bought him for $ 25,000
1936 – 1951:	played for New York Yankees; a great player, could bat and play in the field
1939:	married actress Dorothy Arnold
1954:	married for second time – to Marilyn Monroe, got divorced from her 274 days after he married her; had more success in sports; brother Dom said, "He had everything, but not the right woman to share his life with."
1999:	sick for a long time; died on March 8

4   **Speaking: How do they feel?**

Work in pairs. One of you is the person in one of the photos. The other one must talk to the person. Talk about how he / she feels and why he / she feels that way. Think about feelings like happiness, expectation, surprise and sympathy. Have you got any advice for the person in the picture?

 1   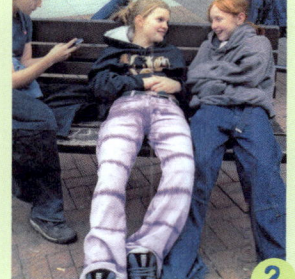 2    3    4

5   **Mediation: Seedfolks**

Your English teacher wants to read Seedfolks in class. She gave you a short text about it. Your mom wants to know what the book is about. Her English is not very good. Tell her about the book in German. Use your exercise book.

In Paul Fleischman's novel *Seedfolks* there is an empty area next to some houses in Cleveland, Ohio. But the place is full of trash and there are lots of rats[9]. It does not look like a place for a garden, especially not to a neighborhood of people who do not know each other and do not seem to care[10]. Until, one day, a young girl starts to clean the place up and plants some seeds. Suddenly this city land that people had forgotten looks hopeful: to Curtis[11] (he thinks he can win back a girl's love); to Virgil's[12] dad (he grows vegetables and thinks he can earn a lot of money); and even to a sixteen-year-old girl (she is expecting a baby and wants to die). Thirteen very different voices – old, young, strong, weak, some scared, others with hope – tell one amazing story about a garden that completely changes a neighborhood.

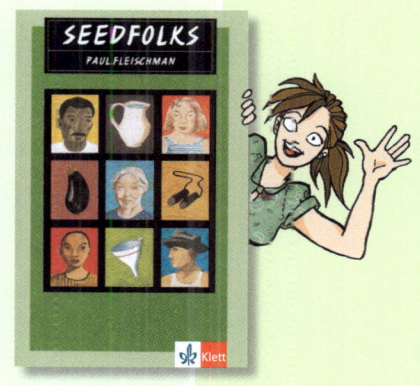

---

[4]**Di Maggio** [dɪˈmædʒɪəʊ] • [5]**profile** [ˈprəʊfaɪl] = Profil, Porträt • [6]**Sicily** [ˈsɪsli] = Sizilien • [7]**Martinez** [mɑːˈtiːnez] •
[8]**seal** [siːl] = Seehund • [9]**rat** [ræt] = Ratte • [10]**to care** [keə] = um etwas kümmern • [11]**Curtis** [ˈkɜːrtɪs] • [12]**Virgil** [ˈvɜːrdʒl]

Unit 2   Go, Bears, go!

> Do the exercises on this page (Choice A) or the exercises on the next page (Choice B).

1 **More news from Berry Middle School** *(Choice A)*   (→ PB p. 32)

a) *The newsletter team is preparing* The Growl *for next month. Here are the beginnings of three articles. Read them, then look at the other parts of the articles. Match them with the right article and put them in the right order. There are three parts for each article.*

A _____   B _____   C _____

_____   _____   _____

A1 | Friday December 10 is the big day for Dustin Joseph and his team. They say they're sure to win the game against

B1 | Here's a photo of some happy winners! These students are relaxing in Greenmount Park after all their hard

C1 | *The Growl* is always full of good news, but sometimes we have to report things which went wrong. This time it's a broken

_____ nothing like that happens at the next fun event, the Winter Dance.

_____ window, two fights and a call to the police, – all in one evening, at the Fall Dance. Not an evening to

_____ Festival last month. "It's great fun, and we are looking for some new young

_____ members," says solo singer Kylee Thomas. Come and listen to the choir at the Winter Concert on December 15!

_____ work. They're just a few of the singers in the BMS choir who won first place in the Music in the Parks

_____ the guys in the team need YOU, too. So come and cheer for the Bears. *Go, fight, win!*

_____ Water Park Middle School, – and they're going to wear their cool new uniforms in the school colors. Our

_____ be proud of, no way, and it brought suspension for four students. (No more dances for them.) Let's make sure

_____ fantastic cheer-leaders will be there to do their chants and their breath-taking stunts, but

b) *Find a heading for each article and write it on the lines above the text.*

2 **Your turn: A text for** *The Growl (Choice A)*   (→ PB p. 32)

Write a short text for The Growl *about sports teams* **or** *music groups* **or** *dances and discos at your school in Germany. Use your exercise book.*

1 Who thinks what? (Choice B) (→ PB p. 35)

a) Read the text on pages 34–35 in your book again.
Put the students' stories in the right order. Write the correct name (Jose, Tiffany, Brittany) in each box,
then give numbers to the parts of each person's story: 1, 2, 3, …

_____

The next day at school Jose's friend Josh told me that Jose was going to the dance with Brittany. I was so angry! And I had told her all my secrets! Just you wait, Brittany Kolden!"

_____

'Send him a pencil and ask him to the dance!' On delivery day I saw Jose, so I asked him about the pencil. Then he told *me*, 'I'll go.' That was crazy.

Jose | 1

"I didn't feel so excited about the Fall Dance. I wasn't the guy all the girls wanted a date with. So I didn't know what to think when I got that pencil. I hadn't sent any. Then Brittany asked me,

_____

I thought, 'Why shouldn't I ask him?' I talked to Brittany about it and she said, 'Yeah, send him a pencil! He'll be so excited.' So I sent him a pencil with a little note. That evening I called him at home, and he reacted like an idiot.

_____

But she was so strange, and she talked about Scott, that football guy. I just didn't understand. One hour later I saw Tiffany. Man, was she angry with Brittany! But I had a bad feeling that it all had to do with me …"

Brittany | 1

"Don't remind me about the Fall Dance! I almost lost my best friend. Tiffany and I talked a lot about the dance. She didn't have a date, and she asked me what I thought of Jose. I guess he's a nice guy, so I told her,

_____

He didn't even say 'Thank you!' for the pencil. I had to tell him about what flowers he should get, and where. But I just thought, 'I guess he's shy.'

_____

Then Tiffany came up to me, really angry. She thought I had asked Jose to the dance! I told her it wasn't true. When she was calm again, suggested we should talk to Jose about it – together!"

Tiffany | 1

"Jose is a really nice guy. His clothes style isn't the best, but he plays in the band, and that's cool. When the Fall Dance was coming closer,

_____

and she wanted to talk to me about her flowers! That could only mean I had *two* dates for the Fall Dance! The next day I asked Brittany about her dress. (I knew all about flowers and other nice things I could say.)

_____

Why didn't he tell Tiffany? The next day it got better – or worse. Jose asked *me* about my outfit! That was something I didn't understand because I had already asked Scott.

_____

'Did you get the pencil?' So *she* knew somebody had sent me one! And then there was her name (well, part of it) on the note! I was sure I had a date with her! Then there was the phone call from Tiffany,

b) Find a heading for each story.

Jose's story: _____

Tiffany's story: _____

Brittany's story: _____

2 Your turn: American schools (Choice B) (→ PB p. 35)

a) Find four things about American schools which are different from German schools in The fall dance. Use your exercise book.

b) Which of these things would you like to have at your school? Why? Prepare a short talk and present it in class.

SPEAKING SKILLS

3 **Get ready to talk**   (→ PB p. 36)

You are going to discuss this topic in a group of four students:

We should have more sports competitions between different schools, like American schools.

Read what some students have said about this topic.
Put these arguments for and against more sports competitions in the list below. Write notes. Then add your own arguments.

"If it's a city or state competition, it's too important for everybody to win." ✔	"It's a great free-time activity to cheer your school team. – Better than TV or computer games." ✔	"I wouldn't like to stand on the side of the sports field for hours in winter!"
"Many of our students already play in competitions for a team at their sports club."	"Students who aren't so good at tests can be heroes in sports competitions."	"If we had competitions between schools, we could have cheerleaders, too!"

for	against
– great free-time activity	– too important to win

4 **Learn how to present your arguments**   (→ PB p. 36)

What phrases can you use to present your arguments, to agree / disagree with others?
Look at page 36 in your book and write a list.

5 **Have a discussion**   (→ PB p. 36)

Two students in your group are for more sports competitions between different schools, two are against it. Prepare your arguments, and then discuss your ideas. Start like this:

A: Now, I'm sure you'll agree that sports competitions are fun for all students.
B: Yes, you're right, but don't forget that many students are members of …

6 Use modal auxiliaries with the perfect infinitive (→ PB p. 38; Grammar → PB G7)

Tiffany does not tell her mother everything about her plans and her friends.
What does Tiffany's mother think?

Use must / might have • needn't have • should / shouldn't have • can't have.

1. "She <u>must have got</u>　　　　　　　　　　　　　　　　　　　　 !"　(detention)

2. "She _____ ."　(jacket)

3. "I _____ ."　(meal)

4. "She _____ !"　(love)

7 The passive infinitive with 'to'　(→ PB p. 39; Grammar → PB G8)

It is almost time for the Winter Dance. Everybody is really excited. Write down what they say or think.

Use expect • would like • hope • want *and the passive infinitive.*

1. Maya: "I hope somebody will invite me to the dance."

　<u>Maya hopes</u> _____

2. Teacher: "You must bring all the food to school before 2 pm."

　<u>The teacher</u> _____

3. Jake and Kelly: "We're sure they'll give us first place in the dancing competition."

　_____

4. Taylor: "Will all the girls ignore me? I wouldn't like that!"

　_____

5. Victoria: "I know the teachers will stop any fights."

　_____

6. Brittany: "I guess Scott will drive me home after the dance."

　_____

8   What must / must not be done?   (→ PB p. 39; Grammar → PB G8)

*Jose decided to get a job. Today is his first day at a Mesquite music store.
He does not do everything right, and Fiona is trying to help him.*

a) *Read what Fiona says to Jose. Underline the rules she tells him.*

"Everything OK with the CDs, Jose? Just a minute. Where are all those cool new discs? At the BACK?
No, no, Jose, <u>you mustn't put the new CDs at the back of the shop</u>. Put them here!
Now, look here, Jose, we've got these cool Disney posters. You can give one free to kids, OK?
Oh no! Look at those guys with their ice-cream! No food in here. That's the rule for you, too, Jose!
There's something important here in the office. The safety rules for everyone who is working here.
Please read them carefully!
Hey, what's that terrible noise? Your cell phone? No, sorry Jose, you can't use your phone in the
store. – That's all. It's easy, isn't it? And if you have any problems, just inform the manager.
Can you remember all that? I guess we ought to make a list of rules. Why don't you make a list and
hang it on my office door?"

b) *Write down the new list of rules in your exercise book. Use modals and passive infinitives.*
   Start like this: 1. New CDs must not be …

9   Mediation: News from Nash Middle School

*A friend in the US has sent you this article about their school theater group from his school newsletter.
Your friend Tina is in your school's theater group and is interested in the article. Her English is not very
good. Answer her questions in German.*

Nash Middle School Production Coming Soon!

The script has been chosen for the school play in February. It's going to be *Oliver
Twist*, so we're looking for students to play the roles of poor kids, rich ladies and
dangerous criminals. Maybe you'd like to audition for the cast of our exciting and
ambitious drama. Auditions will be in November. All students are welcome to audition.
There will be about 30 students in the cast. The successful students' names will be
announced and scripts will be handed out next month. Rehearsals begin in December,
and performances of the play will be on February 14 and 15 in the school hall. If
you'd like to take part but aren't wild about being on stage, how about helping the
crew? We're looking for people to work on make-up and costumes, paint scenery,
make programs and do any number of other jobs! If you're interested, come to the
meeting on November 23. Mark it in your calendar now!

1. Steht in dem Newsletter etwas über eine bevorstehende Aufführung?

   _____

   TIP

   Don't translate the
   text, just give the most
   important information.

2. Wie werden die Rollen verteilt und wie viele Schauspieler brauchen sie?

   _____

3. Kann man da auch mitmachen, ohne auf der Bühne zu stehen?

   _____

4. Wo und wann wird das Stück dann aufgeführt?

   _____

WRITING TEXTS

10 Research the topic (→ PB p. 40)

You are going to write a pro and con text on this topic:

Should students be allowed to give their teachers grades?

Collect ideas for and against grades for teachers in the grid.
Is your text going to be for or against grades for teachers?

for	against
– fair: teachers give grades to students	– Students do not know enough about teachers' work

11 Create a clear structure (→ PB p. 40)

Fill in the grid.

1. title
2. introduction
3. first argument for
4. second argument for
5. first argument against
6. second argument against
7. final argument for / against
8. conclusion

12 Write your text (→ PB p. 40)

a) *Use your plan to write your text in your exercise book.*

b) *Show the text to a classmate and ask for his or her opinion.*
   Are your arguments clear? Try to improve your text.

13 Put in *but, and, so* or *because*   (→ PB p. 41)

Football games are won by the players, of course, _____

the cheerleaders are very important, too. They do gymnastics at games,

_____ they also shout chants. It's not easy to become a

cheerleader _____ you must be fit – and good at school.

Cheerleaders have to practice a lot, _____ they don't have much

time for other hobbies. Cindy wants to be a cheerleader, _____

she's practicing hard. She couldn't join the team last year _____

she was too young. Cindy hopes to get into the team this year, _____ she knows it

won't be easy.

14 School words: An e-mail from Texas   (→ PB p. 41)

Write down the missing words.

What's new this year? Well, I'm in 8th _g_____ now, there are ten new teachers – and we

have a new _p_____ , Mrs. Alvares. We don't wear uniforms, but we have a very strict

_d_____ . Students who ignore it get _d_____ ! They must stay at school after

the 8th _p_____ . My favorite _c_____ ? That's Science. I love it, but no school

would be even better. I'm looking forward to _v_____ at the end of December!

15 Word stress

Say the words and find the stress. Write the words in the correct group.
(Look at the examples.)

advantage   argument ✔   disagree   department   conclusion   furious

recommend   understand   discussion   politics   obvious   interrupt

● ● ●
newsletter

argument_____

_____

_____

_____

● ● ●
remember

_____

_____

_____

_____

● ● ●
introduce

_____

_____

_____

_____

16 **Use modal verbs and the perfect infinitive** (→ PB p. 42; Grammar → PB G7)

Kelly is waiting for her boyfriend outside a café.
What does she think in these situations?

1. Her boyfriend Zack has not arrived for their date.

   (can't • forget)   " _He can't_____ "

2. It is getting cold outside.

   (should • wear)   "_____ "

3. Her cell phone is not in her bag.

   (must • leave)   "_____ "

4. Zack arrives with flowers and says, "Sorry, I'm late."

   (should • be patient) "_____ "

17 **The passive infinitive** (→ PB p. 42; Grammar → PB G8)

Cody: "I hope they'll choose me for the team." **1**

Tiffany: "I hope somebody will invite me to the dance." **2**

Brittany: "Maybe Mom and Dad will take me out for dinner." **3**

Jose: "I guess they'll pay me well for my work here." **4**

Use want • would like • expect • hope *with the passive infinitive.*

1. _Cody hopes_____

2. _____

3. _____

4. _____

18 **Use modals and the passive infinitive** (→ PB p. 42; Grammar → PB G8)

What information do these pictures give?

 **1**  **2**  **3**  **4**

1. _____

2. _____

3. _____

4. _____

⟨Revision⟩ Unit 1–2

1 Mixed bag

What a semester! I __joined__ the gymnastics team, but I must admit – I _____ really do very

well. Well, maybe I should have _____ a bit more … I was better in Student _____.

I thought _____ some great arguments against the new _____ – but it didn't help. The

principal still ignored _____ arguments and from next semester on _____ will all have to

read thousands of _____ before we can put on our clothes in the morning!

I didn't expect to get brilliant _____ – especially in English – and I was right. I was really sad

_____ I love English. But it was always the first period, and so I _____ it half the time!

Of course, I often got _____, so the day started and _____ later for me than for most

people. But the important thing is … Yes, I got a date _____ the school dance with a really cool

_____. What a semester!

2 Mike's date!

Mike has a date with Katie, but something has gone wrong. Look at the pictures and write sentences.
Use a modal auxiliary with the perfect infinitive of the verbs under the pictures.

1. Mike __should_____ earlier. It's 4:30 already.

2. Katie _____ again already.

3. Mike _____ and told her he would be late.

4. He _____.

3 Do you want to be a cheerleader?

*Complete the text with the verbs in the passive infinitive with or without **to**.*

Everybody who would like _to be given_ (give) the chance to join our cheerleading team

can come to the try-outs next Saturday. But remember! To be a cheerleader, a lot of hard work

has _____ (do) every week. New stunts have _____ (practice)

and new chants must _____ (learn). Don't come to the try-outs because you hope

_____ (ask) on a date by a football player. We always get some cheerleaders who only

do it because they expect _____ (invite) to great parties all year. Of course, we may

_____ (invite) to parties sometimes, but often we don't have time to go. And don't believe

anything else that may _____ (say)!

4 I was a cheerleader

*Complete the text with past perfect progressive forms and **since** or **for**.*

I _____ (go) to try-outs _____

years before they finally asked me to become a cheerleader.

Curtis and I _____ (sit) in the same

class at school _____ first grade, but he had never noticed me. Curtis never thought about

anything else apart from football. I _____ (cheer) at a game _____

15 minutes when he finally noticed me. And everybody else noticed me, too. The other cheerleaders

were jumping to the right when I jumped to the left and we all fell over. How embarrassing! I

_____ (wait) for this moment _____ three years, but now I hope

Curtis never notices me again.

5 Jobs, jobs, jobs!

With your partner discuss the following sentence:

It is good to work while you are still at school.

The following steps and the Speaking skills on p. 36 in your book can help you.

1. *First decide who is going to be for and against this.*
2. *Collect arguments and write down Useful phrases.*
3. *Discuss your ideas.*

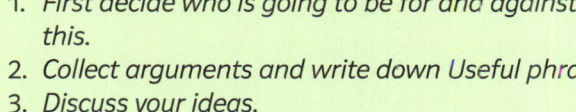

You've already finished the first two units of Green Line 4 – well done! Fill in your *Portfolio* – what went well, and what could still be improved?

Unit 3   Out West

1   The American West   (→ PB p. 46)

A

B

a) *Decide who is A and who is B. Partner A looks at picture A and writes the beginning of a story for picture A. Partner B writes the beginning of a story for picture B.*

b) *Take your partner's story and write an ending to it. Use your exercise book.*

2   Western crossword   (→ PB p. 46)

1. The Grand Canyon is in this state.
2. A state with some of the "world's best snow".
3. Many Indian tribes live on a …
4. You can ride wild horses here.
5. The American West starts at this river.
6. This is a famous area for skiers in the US: … Mountains
7. Mt. McKinley is in this state.
8. This is another name for Indians: … Americans
9. The … West

3   Listening: Why are they in Jackson?   (→ PB p. 47)

Right, wrong or not in the text?

	right	wrong	not in the text
1. Native Americans were some of the first "mobile" people.	☐	☐	☐
2. Tennessee is not like Wyoming.	☐	☐	☐
3. Dustin's parents are divorced.	☐	☐	☐
4. Dustin lived in Boston for a year.	☐	☐	☐
5. Ritchie is Dean's best friend.	☐	☐	☐
6. Dustin's mom loves country music.	☐	☐	☐

4 Gerunds (→ PB p. 49; Grammar → PB G9)

Underline the sentences. Use blue for the sentences with gerund as an object, red for the sentences with gerund as a subject and green for the sentences with gerund after a preposition.

1. <u>I enjoy eating at the lodge.</u>
2. I'm crazy about shopping.
3. Do you feel like dancing?
4. I'm good at playing soccer.

5. Driving in the mountains is dangerous.
6. She worries about getting bad grades.
7. Waiting for snow is the worst.
8. I love walking in the snow.

5 Gerunds as subject or object (→ PB p. 49; Grammar → PB G9)

Write a sentence about each picture with gerund as the subject or as the object.

1. Sylvia _____ .

2. Dean _____ .

3. _____
   is Ritchie's dream.

4. _____
   is Dean's weekend job.

6 Listening: Getting to Jackson (→ PB p. 49)

Right, wrong or not in the text?

	right	wrong	not in the text
1. It is a live conversation.	☐	☐	☐
2. Skiing is the main tourist activity here in winter.	☐	☐	☐
3. It is easy to get to Jackson airport.	☐	☐	☐
4. Jackson has a nice station.	☐	☐	☐
5. You cannot talk to a tourist agent.	☐	☐	☐
6. The airport is just a few miles outside of town.	☐	☐	☐

7 Around Jackson (→ PB p. 49; Grammar → PB G9)

a) *Dustin and his mom want to visit the area around Jackson.*
Put the words together to complete the sentences with gerund constructions.

Mom: The mountains feel safe when it's sunny. But I'm ___worried about driving___

(worried about • drive) when it's snowing.

Dustin: Dean says you soon _____ (get used to • watch) the weather.

Mom: Hm, yes, I guess he's right. I don't _____ (feel like • get)

lost in a snow storm in the mountains. I don't know anything about mountains!

Dustin: Well, Mom, remember how you were _____ (look

forward to • buy) a new car? Let's get a jeep. Mountains, here we come!

Mom: Not so fast. I've been _____ (think of • talk) to Dean's

dad about the best kind of car out here. I met him in town last week.

Dustin: I'm _____ (tired of • talk) about the mountains. I want to get

up there.

Mom: I'm just as _____ (excited about • go) up there as you

are, but I'm also _____ (interested in • get) the best

information for our safety.

Dustin: OK, OK. I'll _____ (give up • try) to convince you.

b) *How would you say these sentences with gerund constructions in German?*

8 Mediation: Tourism in Jackson

Jackson Hole Wildlife Safaris offers many tours. Two German tourists (whose English is not very good) try to read a brochure. They ask you to help them and tell them the most important things in German. Use your exercise book.

TIP

Just give the most important information. Use your own words.

Welcome to *Jackson Hole Wildlife Safaris*. We've been offering wildlife and photography safaris for 40 years. Our guides lead their safaris with years of experience and first-hand knowledge of the area that can only come from living and breathing Jackson Hole. The tours include finding and safely photographing wildlife, historic buildings and different kinds of landscape. We are good at making our guests feel great. All of our trips include hot beverages (especially teas and hot chocolate), snacks and a water bottle for you to keep. We are famous for serving a European style picnic lunch on full-day tours with homemade cookies for dessert. And sitting around the campfire at night with our guides for a scary ghost story about Jackson's secret past is always a highlight for visitors. So join us in creating your perfect wildlife safari in and around Jackson Hole.

9 **Explaining with gerunds**   (→ PB p. 50: Grammar → PB G9)

Sylvia has moved to Jackson. She has invited her friends to visit her. Use gerund constructions to say what Sylvia's friends say. Use the words below and be careful with the tenses.

| start | couldn't imagine ✔ | look forward to | love ✔ |

1. Susie: It's really great to ski with my friends.

   Susie _loves skiing with her friends._

2. Kate: I've never lived in a small town. I don't think I could imagine it.

   Kate _couldn't imagine_

3. Lin: I can't wait to see the Rocky Mountains.

   Lin _____

4. Matt: I skied for the first time two years ago. Jackson here I come!

   Matt _____

10 **Make sentences with objects and *ing*-forms**   (→ PB p. 50; Grammar → PB G10)

look forward to • parents • meet • Dean • soon

always look forward to • Dean • call me

miss • Sylvia • hold my hand

don't like • Dean • drive up the mountains • snow

hate • Dean and Ritchie • spend • so much time • together

love • Sylvia • tell me

1. Sylvia: _"I'm looking forward to my parents meeting Dean soon."_

2. Sylvia: _"I always look forward_

3. Dean: _____

4. Sylvia: _____

5. Sylvia: _____

6. Dean: _____

TALKWISE

11 **Say it politely** (→ PB p. 51)

a) *Underline the most polite sentence and write down where the conversation takes place.*

1. a) Give me the salad, please.
   b) <u>Could I have the salad, please?</u>
   c) I want the salad!

   at home / in a restaurant

2. a) I can't find my size.
   b) Hey, you don't have my size.
   c) Excuse me, but I can't find my size.

   _____

3. a) My noodles are all gone.
   b) I don't have any noodles.
   c) Could I please have some more noodles?

   _____

4. a) I'm afraid you don't have any more apples.
   b) I wanted some apples – and you don't have any.
   c) Aren't you ever going to get more apples out here?

   _____

5. a) You can answer the phone.
   b) You could answer the phone for me, you know.
   c) Would you mind answering the phone for me, please?

   _____

b) *Make conversations with a partner. Use the correct sentences from a) and your own polite answers.*

12 **Partner activity: Small talk in a store** (→ PB p. 51)

Partner A works in a clothes store and partner B is a customer.
React to the sentences / questions below and then go on with the
polite small talk. Use the information from the box.
The tip below and the Useful phrases on p. 51 in your book can help you.

TIP

A smile and a friendly
face help a lot in small
talk situations.

A: Hi, how are you today? B: …

A: Can I help you? B: …

A: Oh, I'm sorry, but we B: …
haven't got shorts.
Why do you need shorts
in November?

Go on, please.

A
- has no shorts in winter
- loves Mexico
- never been to Germany

B
- looking for shorts
- vacation to Mexico
- German exchange student

TIP

Try these tips to make things sound more polite:

Use the word 'please'.	• Close the door, please.
Use a question.	• Do you think you could …? • Could you please …?
Apologize.	• I'm sorry, but there aren't any more … • Excuse me, but I can't find the …
Show that you are interested.	• I'd love to hear more about … • Can you tell me some more about …? • Wow! • I see. • Really? • Oh, my!

13 **Native Americans and the 'New World'**   (→ PB p. 52; Grammar → PB G11)

Underline the passive forms.

When Europeans first came to the 'New World', there were probably millions of Native Americans. But it was not long before they were pushed away to the west. Their lands were sold to settlers. But this was not all. The Indians were even killed because the settlers were afraid of them.

By the 1800s, a lot of land was being given to white settlers by the government – land that had been taken away from the Native Americans. Indian reservations were being created and the Indians had to move there. But the reservations were often far away from where the Indians had lived before, and the land was often bad, or there were not enough buffalo in the area.

There were many wars between Americans and Native Americans. The last battle was the Battle of Wounded Knee[1]. 300 Native American men, women and children were killed.

The problems between the Native Americans and the European settlers are still being discussed today by their great-great-great-grandchildren. Solutions to the problems cannot always be found, but the American government is more interested in trying than ever before.

14 **Describe the pictures with the present progressive passive**   (PB p. 52; Grammar → PB G12)

pack **1**

move **2**

build **3**

found **4**

open **5**

close **6**

1. The covered wagon is being packed. _____

2. The Native Americans _____

3. _____

4. _____

5. _____

6. _____

[1]**Wounded Knee** [ˌwuːndɪd ˈniː] = Name eines historischen Massakers

15 Miss Navajo Nation   (→ PB p. 53; Grammar → PB G12)

Put in the correct passive progressive forms in this text about 'Miss Navajo Nation', Lillie Kanti.

It is not always easy to find the right person for the role of Miss Navajo Nation. During our interviews with different Navajo tribe members we ___were being told___ (tell) that a Miss Navajo Nation must speak both English and Navajo. But the Navajo language _____(speak) by fewer and fewer people. However, this was not a problem for this year's Miss Navajo Nation, Lillie Kanti. She _____ (teach) the Navajo language by the time she was 5.

Her grandmother played an important role in her education. "Learning is very important to me because it means I _____ (give) the chance to speak for my people," Lillie reported. "The Miss Navajo Nation Competition is another way to speak for my people."

During the whole history of white people in North America, the Navajo people could not decide for themselves where and how to live. With this competition, the Navajo tribe _____ (give) the chance to discover its traditions again. Navajo children _____ (show) that they can be happy to be part of the Navajo Nation. "I'm so happy to be Miss Navajo Nation and proud to be a Navajo," Lillie said with the biggest smile west of the Mississippi.

16 Chicago   (→ PB p. 53; Grammar → PB G11, 12)

Underline the passive forms in the correct tense.

People on the move! That is what Chicago is all about. It (has been known • will be known • was known) for its transport since its beginning. Chicago (is being founded • was founded • had been founded) in the 1830s near the Chicago River and the place (was chosen • were chosen • has been chosen) because it was perfect for trade[1]. Then plans (were being made • will be made • had not been made) to link the Chicago and Mississippi Rivers and in 1848 this (will be completed • will have been completed • was completed). Through Chicago the east and the west (has been linked • was linked • had been linked). After the railroad (were built • will be built • had been built) in 1848, Chicago became even more important for linking east and west. Soon 100 trains came and went every day. And today the trains (were still used • will be used • are still being used).

         [1]**trade** [treɪd] = Handel

GRAMMAR SKILLS

17 **Do you know these grammar words?** (→ PB p. 54)

Follow the commands and change the sentences.

1. *Add an adverb of degree:* I enjoy my job as a waiter at the lodge.

   _____

2. *Change since to for:* I have been working there since October. It is January now.

   _____

3. *Use a gerund in this sentence:* I don't mind if I have to work extra hours on the weekend.

   _____

4. *Change to the passive voice:* We give our best customers a table at the window.

   _____

5. *Change to the passive voice:* My parents are paying for my room at the lodge.

   _____

18 **Which learner type are you?** (→ PB p. 54)

Read the list of different ways you can learn things.
How useful are they to you: very useful, sometimes useful, not useful?
Put a tick ✔ in the boxes.

> **TIP**
> Find out the best way for you to learn things. Learning is much easier if you know which type you are.

	very useful	sometimes useful	not useful
1. Trying to find out the rules for new grammar.	☐	☐	☐
2. Reading a comic which explains new things.	☐	☐	☐
3. Listening to my teacher while he / she explains new things.	☐	☐	☐
4. Looking at the pictures and texts in my book.	☐	☐	☐
5. Making my own example sentences for new grammar.	☐	☐	☐
6. Watching a film about a new topic.	☐	☐	☐
7. Making a grid with the things I have to learn.	☐	☐	☐
8. Listening to my partner while he / she explains something.	☐	☐	☐
9. Making rhymes with new things.	☐	☐	☐
10. Organizing things I have to learn in a mind map.	☐	☐	☐

Most (very useful) ticks for numbers 1, 5, 10: The best way for you to learn things is to think about them.
Most (very useful) ticks for numbers 3, 8, 9: The best way for you to learn things is to listen to them.
Most (very useful) ticks for numbers 2, 4, 6, 7: The best way for you to learn things is to look at / read about them.

19 Shane's article about the Skywalk (→ PB p. 58)

a) *Answer the questions in note form:*

1. Where is the Skywalk?

   _____

   _____

2. Who built it? _____

   _____

3. Why was it built? _____

4. What does it look like? _____

   _____

5. What is good about the Skywalk? _____

   _____

   _____

6. What is bad about it?_____

   _____

b) *Writing texts: Write Shane's newspaper article. Use your notes from a).*
   The tips below can help you.

WRITING SKILLS

Writing a newspaper article

Follow these steps.

Headline: Your headline should get people's attention and tell readers what the article is about. Use the story for ideas.

Beginning: Start with the basic information. Answer some or all of these questions: *who, what, when and where.*

The main point: Decide what the main point of Shane's article is.
Is he for or against the Skywalk? Is it good or bad?

More details: Then give more details about *who, what, when, where, why* and *how*.

Background information: Give the reader some background information on the topic.

Remember:
- Don't give your opinion in a newspaper article.
- Often the passive is used in newspaper reports when you don't know who did the action or if it's not important.
- It's important to use direct speech to write exactly what people said.

Grand Canyon or Disneyland?

The Skywalk was built by the Hualapai tribe at the Grand Canyon Resort.
…

20 Listening: BE or AE? (→ PB p. 59)

a) *Listen to the sentences on the CD. Decide if the sentence is American English or British English. Put a tick* ✔ *in the right box.*

Sentence	American English	British English	Which word(s) tell(s) you this?
1.	☐	✔	underground, aunt
2.	☐	☐	
3.	☐	☐	
4.	☐	☐	
5.	☐	☐	
6.	☐	☐	

b) *Listen again. Write down the word(s) which tell(s) you this.*

21 Word groups

Underline the wrong word in the groups and then give each group a title.

1. Hualapai • French • Kaw • Sioux _____

2. reservation • tribe • settler • Indian _____

3. lodge • covered wagon • shopping mall • gas station _____

4. slope • rodeo • war • fishing _____

22 How to: Be more positive! (→ PB p. 59)

a) *Use polite phrases to make the conversation between a tourist (A) and a shop assistant (B) more positive. The Useful phrases on page 59 in your book can help you. Use your exercise book.*

A: Hello. I want two of these postcards. I only found one.

B: They're here. Look.

A: I need stamps to send the postcards to Germany.

B: How many?

A: Two.

B: I know Germany.

A: Really?

B: Yes. That's $2.50.

A: Here you are. Goodbye.

B: Goodbye.

b) *Act the conversation out with a partner.*

23 Put in the gerunds (→ PB p. 60; Grammar → PB G9)

| fish | see | go | listen | ski | visit | ride | relax |

The winters in Jackson are great, but have you seen our summers? If you like _____ in the mountains, you will love _____ on hikes in them in the summer, too. Or maybe _____ a horse is more your thing! Or if you just enjoy _____ in the fresh mountain air, _____ to a concert at our music festival in July is a great idea. _____ in our mountain rivers is another popular activity. Many tourists spend their whole vacation _____ the national parks near Jackson. We look forward to _____ you in Jackson – at any time of the year!

24 Choose the correct prepositions

I had always dreamed _____ meeting Mr. Right. But I was not very good _____ meeting new people. And I was tired _____ going on dates with friends of friends. Then one day I was at the supermarket and I was just talking to the cashier _____ the weather. He told me he loved skiing and did not feel _____ spending another winter without snow and mountains. I told him I was interested _____ skiing, too, and thinking _____ moving to a new place with mountains. It was so easy to talk to him and I did not even worry _____ sounding strange. That was two years ago and now John and I live in Jackson, Wyoming, with lots of snow and mountains. So my advice is: keep _____ dreaming and do not give _____ hoping! You can look forward _____ meeting your Mr. or Mrs. Right, too!

25 Complete the sentences with object + *ing*-forms (→ PB p. 60; Grammar → PB G10)

1. Dean is out in the car. Now it's snowing. I'm worried about …

   _____

2. Dustin has invited his friends to his house. He is looking forward to …

   _____

3. Ritchie's parents always tell him to get good grades. He hates …

   _____

4. Sylvia gets e-mails from her friends every night. She loves …

   _____

26 Change from active to passive   (→ PB p. 61; Grammar → PB G11, 12)

1. People are thinking about Route 66 in a whole new way.

   Route 66 is _____

2. They took Route 66 off the maps in 1985.

   _____

3. People have called it the 'Mother Road'.

   _____

4. They are planning a Route 66 car show in California.

   _____

27 A student's report   (→ PB p. 61)

Read a student's report about Zion[1] National Park. There are things in the report which could be improved. Underline them and write down what should be changed.

<u>I think it is amazing</u> that <u>snow and ice made</u> the landscape of Zion National Park. Over millions of years the Virgin River carved out Zion Canyon. The really cool pictures that you can see in some

5 of the rocks were carved out or painted by the Indians.

In 1917 the first lodge was built and two years later – I think – Zion National Park was founded. More visitors visit this national park than any

10 other national park in Utah. In 1930 people completed the Zion-Mt. Carmel[2] Highway, which is 14 miles long.

They offer hikes at the park and that is a good thing because I like hikes.

Line 1 : _don't give your own opinion, use the passive_ _____

_____ : _____

_____ : _____

_____ : _____

_____ : _____

_____ : _____

_____ : _____

[1]**Zion** ['zaɪən] • [2]**Carmel** ['kaːrmel]

〈The ransom[1]〉

It was a Wednesday afternoon, at around 4:30 p.m., I guess, when the kid first came to my office. 'McGill', it says on the door. 'J. McGill. Private Detective'. Not a bad job. It's difficult
5 sometimes, I admit, but I like it. From my office, I can see right over Boston Harbor to Charlestown Bridge. It was a beautiful October day, I remember. The sun was shining through my window.

10 "You've got to help me, Mr. McGill! You –"
"Now wait a minute!" The kid was scared. I noticed that the moment he came into my office. "Keep cool, kid. Let's start at the beginning. What's your name?"
15 "Nelson Wainwright[2]. You know my brother Steve, right?"
"Oh? Steve Wainwright? Yeah, I remember him, sure." So Nelson here was the younger of the Wainwright brothers. Their father owned the
20 Wainwright Company. Rich, very rich. I knew Steve from a few years ago, when we'd played baseball together. I looked at the kid in front of me. How old was he? Twenty, twenty-one maybe?
"OK, Nelson, so what's wrong? Have you left
25 home?" He was carrying a small suitcase[3], I noticed.
"No, Mr. McGill. It's my girlfriend. She –"
"Call me Butch. Everybody else does. – So, what's this about your girlfriend?"
30 "She's been kidnapped[4]! And the kidnappers want a ransom of half a million dollars! I have to give them the money by tomorrow night. They –"
"Wait a minute, Nelson. Your girlfriend has been kidnapped? And you have to pay the
35 kidnappers? That sounds a bit strange. Why don't the kidnappers try to get the money from her parents?" "Gloria doesn't have any parents. They died years ago. And they weren't rich, anyway."
Unlike[5] the Wainwrights, I thought. "OK," I
40 said. "Now tell me, when did this happen?"
"Last night. Gloria told me that she was going out with some friends and that she would call me when she got back to her apartment. But she never did! And this morning I got this phone call
45 from the kidnappers."
"And you don't have any idea who these kidnappers might be?"
"No, Butch. All I know is that they're going to

kill Gloria if they don't get their money. I've got to make sure they get it. I've got to get her back and 50 save her!"
He put the suitcase down on a chair. "The money's in there. Keep it for me until tomorrow. I –"
"What? You're telling me there's half a million 55 dollars in that suitcase? Are you crazy? Where did you get the money, kid?"
"Out of my father's safe[6]. My parents are away just now – but they may be back at any time! My father would go crazy if he found the money in 60 my room! He doesn't like Gloria. Help me, Butch, please!"
"Who is this girl, Nelson? Gloria who?"
"Hammersmith. That's her name. She –"
"Oh, I know. The fashion model, right? Wasn't 65 she Tony Cavori's girl at one time? From 'Cavori's Pizzeria'?"
"Yeah. But that's history. She's my girl now."
It all seemed a bit strange to me. If it was old Wainwright's money these guys wanted, why 70 didn't they kidnap the boy? But this girl Gloria … it made no sense[7]. But then, here was the kid with the money, and I could see that he was really worried about his girl, so I agreed to help. He said he'd come back the next day to pick up 75 the money and talk about how to hand it over[8] to the kidnappers. When he'd gone, I picked up the phone. I had to make some calls.

Early Thursday evening, Nelson was back. Before I gave him the suitcase we talked. The 80 kidnappers had called again and told him where to come with the money. I said that I would go with him, but he didn't like the idea. "No, Butch! They told me to come alone. I don't want to risk anything. There may be three or four of them – it 85 might be a gang!" "But –"
"No!" Nelson was angry. "It's best for me to do

---

[1]**ransom** ['rænsəm] = money that has to be paid to kidnappers • [2]**Wainwright** ['weɪnraɪt] • [3]**suitcase** ['suːtkeɪs] = bag used for traveling • [4]**to kidnap** ['kɪdnæp] = to take a person and not let him / her go until you get money • [5]**unlike** [ʌn'laɪk] = not like • [6]**safe** [seɪf] = safe place to keep money • [7]**it made no sense** [sens] = *here:* he did not understand • [8]**to hand sth over** [hænd 'əʊvə] = to give sth to sb

this alone. If anything goes wrong, Gloria's life will be in danger. You know that!"

90 "But promise me one thing," I warned him. "Make sure it's a direct exchange⁹ – the money for Gloria. If you give them the money without getting Gloria back, they'll want more and more. Don't forget that, OK?"

95 "OK, don't worry," he answered. He took the suitcase and left.

That night, Nelson called me from his home. The kid was in a panic. It was obvious that something had gone wrong.

100 We can't talk on the phone," I told him. "Stay right where you are. I'll be there in ten minutes."

I knew where he lived. It was up on Beacon¹⁰ Hill, where all the million-dollar houses are. I got in my car and drove down towards 105 Causeway Street, until I came to Beacon Hill. The Wainwrights' house was in a quiet street. Nelson opened the door and I went inside. He was alone.

"Where's Gloria?" I said. "What happened?"

"I went to the place," he began. "It was a 110 phone booth¹¹ on a street corner. But then they called me and told me to go to another place."

"What? So you never saw Gloria? You never met anyone?" It didn't sound good. "No. And I had to leave the money there. They said if I 115 didn't, they'd – "

"But I warned you, kid! You shouldn't have done that!" I shouted. I was angry now.

"I know!" he said. "But they said they needed time to get away. They promised to phone again 120 tomorrow evening at 8 and tell me where I could pick her up."

"And you think they'll still make that phone call? Well, let's hope they do, kid," I said. "I'll come back tomorrow evening and we'll see what 125 happens."

On Friday evening I was back on Beacon Hill. Nelson's parents still hadn't come back. We waited two hours, but the phone didn't ring. That didn't surprise me, of course. The kid was getting more and more nervous. Me, too, because my 130 plan had gone wrong. Finally I had to tell him.

"Nelson," I said. "There's something you don't know. I – er – I still have the money."

"What do you mean?"

"The money in that suitcase – I changed it." 135

"Changed it? What? I don't understand," he said.

"It's quite simple," I said. "I didn't want you and your family to lose all that money – so I changed the bills¹² for forged¹³ ones. I know the 140 right people, you know."

"What?" he shouted. "You put forged bills in the suitcase?" "Yeah, it wasn't perfect, but good enough. It looked OK. I thought the kidnappers wouldn't notice it until they'd let Gloria go. I 145 thought it would be a direct exchange." The kid was furious. "Do you know what that means? You've killed Gloria!" He raised his hand and came over to where I was sitting. He looked very angry. Then the doorbell rang. "Gloria?" He 150 ran out into the hall. He opened the door and I listened.

"Sergeant¹⁴ Kelly, State Police," I heard a man's voice say. "Are you Mr. Nelson Wainwright?"

"That's right. But Gloria …? Have you …?" 155

"Miss Gloria Hammersmith was arrested¹⁵ an hour ago at the airport. She and her friend were trying to buy tickets to Honolulu – with forged bills. We hope that you or your father can help us and answer some questions." 160

"Friend? What friend?" Nelson asked. "Somebody called Cavori. Antonio Cavori. Do you know the guy at all?"

adapted from: *The ransom* by Rosemary Hellyer-Jones

⁹**direct exchange** [daɪ,rekt ɪks'tʃeɪndʒ] = *here:* the money is given to the kidnappers and at the same time and place they give the girl back • ¹⁰**Beacon** ['biːkn] = light • ¹¹**phone booth** ['fəʊn ,buːθ] = phone box • ¹²**bill** [bɪl] = paper money • ¹³**forged** ['fɔːdʒd] = not real • ¹⁴**Sergeant** ['sɑːdʒnt] = Unteroffizier • ¹⁵**to be arrested** [bi ə'restɪd] = to be taken away by the police after a crime

👥 **1** **Before you read**

Which famous detectives do you know and what are they like? Talk to a partner.

2 **Working with the text**

a) *Underline what Butch thinks and how he behaves. Then write a profile in your exercise book.*

b) *Nelson writes a letter to Gloria in prison. What does he say? Use your exercise book.*

👥 c) *In groups of four, write your own detective story: A new adventure for Butch.*

〈Revision for tests〉 Unit 2–3

1 Understanding the text: The Battle at Wounded Knee[1] Creek[2]

In a contract signed at Fort Laramie[3] in 1868, the Indians were given land by the US government which became the Great Sioux Reservation in South Dakota. In the 1870s, however, gold was found there in the Black Hills which was a religious place for the Sioux. More and more white men arrived and the Black Hills War started in 1876. In the following year and after several battles, the US army defeated the Sioux and took land away from them.

In February 1890, even more land was taken away from the Sioux and was given to white farmers. As a result the Indians had to live on five small reservations and send their children to boarding schools where teaching traditional Native American culture and language was not allowed. Although the Native Americans were hunters[4], they could not hunt on the reservation because there were not enough animals. So they had to farm like the white men, but the land was bad for farming and soon there was not enough food. The US government promised to give the Sioux more food and other things they needed, but they did not.

In the fall of 1890, more and more Sioux began to dance the Ghost Dance, an important religious dance. Some white settlers thought it was a war dance and were frightened. They asked the government for protection[5] and soon thousands of soldiers arrived. The Sioux chief[6], Big Foot, really wanted peace. Very ill, he went with his people to Pine Ridge[7] Reservation, but on December 28, 1890, Colonel James Forsyth,[8] and 500 US soldiers on horses stopped them. They had been commanded to catch Big Foot, to search[9] all the Indians for guns and to collect these.

The Sioux chief and about 350 of his people slept that night near a small river called Wounded Knee Creek. The next morning, the soldiers moved in around them and put big guns on the hills above the creek. Big Foot was talking with James Forsyth, when they heard a shot. Most of the Indians had already given their guns to the soldiers, but the medicine man[10] did not want to give his gun to them. A soldier tried to take the gun away from him and the gun went off. Then the Battle at Wounded Knee Creek started. At the end of the fight, Big Foot and at least 150 Sioux men, women and children were dead.

Some say as many as 300 Indians died – and twenty-five soldiers, maybe killed by their own men. About 150 Sioux ran away, but many died in the cold. It was not just a battle, it was a massacre[11] and it is now often called the 'Wounded Knee Massacre'. It was the last battle in the wars between the US government and the Indians.

a) *Put these events in the right order:*

[___] Ghost Dance – [___] massacre – [___] Black Hills War – [___] no food – [___] Wounded Knee

b) *Answer the following questions. First underline important parts in the text, then answer the questions in your exercise book.*

1. Why did the Native Americans have to live on five small reservations?
2. Why was it hard to live on the reservations?
3. Why did the massacre start?

---

[1]**Wounded Knee** [ˌwuːndɪd 'niː] • [2]**creek** [kriːk] = Nebenfluss • [3]**Fort Laramie** [fɔːrt 'lærəmi] • [4]**hunter** ['hʌntə] = Jäger / -in • [5]**protection** [prə'tekʃn] = Schutz • [6]**chief** [tʃiːf] = Häuptling • [7]**Pine Ridge** ['paɪn rɪdʒ] • [8]**Forsyth** ['fɔːrsaɪθ] • [9]**to search** [sɜːtʃ] = durchsuchen • [10]**medicine man** ['medsn mæn] = Medizinmann • [11]**massacre** ['mæsəkə] = Massaker

Auf diesen Seiten findest du noch einmal die wichtigsten Grammatikregeln aus *Green Line* 4. Du kannst den Bogen heraustrennen und so ganz einfach etwas nachschlagen, wenn du deine Hausaufgaben machst oder die Grammatik wiederholst.

G Die Verlaufsform des Perfekts   The present perfect progressive

Das *present perfect* hat, wie alle anderen englischen Zeitformen auch, eine *simple form* und eine *progressive form*.

▶ Mit dem *present perfect progressive* kannst du eine Handlung beschreiben, die in der Vergangenheit angefangen hat und noch nicht beendet ist. Das *present perfect progressive* betont die **Dauer** dieses Vorgangs.
▶ *For* und *since* werden sehr häufig mit dem *present perfect progressive* verwendet.

How long		
Diego **has been cooking**	**for**	three hours.

Since when		
Diego **has been living** in America	**since**	1989.

▶ *For* bezieht sich auf den **Zeitraum**, den eine Handlung andauert.

▶ *Since* bezieht sich auf den **Zeitpunkt**, an dem die Handlung begann.

G Die Verlaufsform des Plusquamperfekts   The past perfect progressive

Die Verlaufsform des Plusquamperfekts beschreibt, wie lange eine Handlung angedauert hatte, bevor eine andere Handlung eintrat.

Diego	**had been dreaming**	of his own business **for ages**	before he opened his diner.
Diego	**has been cooking**	eggs **since the early morning**,	so he felt tired.

▶ Das *past perfect progressive* wird gebildet aus *had + been + present participle*. Es ist für alle Personen gleich.
▶ Oft wird das *past perfect progressive* mit Zeitangaben wie *for*, *since*, *all morning*, *the whole week* etc. verbunden.
▶ Die neu eintretende Handlung steht im *simple past*.

G Modale Hilfsverben mit dem Infinitiv Perfekt
Modal auxiliaries with the perfect infinitive

Wenn du sagen möchtest, was in der **Vergangenheit** hätte geschehen können, sollen oder müssen, kannst du Modalverben zusammen mit dem **Infinitiv Perfekt** verwenden:

Subject	Modal auxiliary	Perfect infinitive	Rest of the sentence
It	**must**	**have been**	a difficult decision for Tiffany.
Es muss eine schwierige Entscheidung für Tiffany gewesen sein.			
She	**should**	**have told**	her mother.
Sie hätte es ihrer Mutter sagen sollen.			

▶ Die Perfektform des Infinitivs wird gebildet aus *have + past participle*: *should have told*, *might have given* etc.

G   Der Infinitiv des Passivs   The passive infinitive

▶ Der Infinitiv Passiv wird gebildet aus **be + past participle** (**be informed**). Er kann mit oder ohne **to** verwendet werden.

a) Der Infinitiv des Passivs mit *to*   *The passive infinitive with* to

Nach Verben wie **hope, would like, want, expect, seem** usw. steht der Infinitiv des Passivs mit **to**.

Subject	Verb	Passive infinitive + to	Rest of the sentence	
Lots of young people	**hope**	**to be discovered**	one day.	… hoffen … entdeckt zu werden.

b) Der Infinitiv des Passivs ohne *to*   *The passive infinitive without* to

Wenn du sagen möchtest, dass etwas getan werden kann, muss oder soll, kannst du ein modales Hilfsverb (**can, must, should** etc.) zusammen mit dem Infinitiv des Passivs verwenden.

Subject	Modal auxiliary	Passive infinitive	Rest of the sentence	
Only a few jobs	**can**	**be found**	in the film industry.	Man kann … finden.

▶ Der Infinitiv des Passivs wird direkt (ohne **to**) an die modalen Hilfsverben **can, may, might** usw. angehängt, z.B. **can be found, might be done**.

▶ Im Deutschen wird diese Konstruktion häufig durch Sätze mit **man** und dem Verb im Aktiv (man kann nicht glauben) wiedergegeben.

G   Das Gerund   The gerund

Genau wie das *present participle* wird das **gerund** aus dem Infinitiv ohne *to* + *-ing* gebildet. Es gelten für das *gerund* auch die gleichen Schreibregeln:

play + ing → playing   swi**m** + ing → swi**mm**ing   driv**e** + ing → dri**v**ing

Das **gerund** ist eine Verbform, die du ähnlich wie ein Nomen verwenden kannst. Im Satz kann das **gerund** verschiedene Funktionen haben.

▶ Das **gerund** kann wie ein Nomen Subjekt des Satzes sein. Vergleiche: **Football** is fun. **Skiing** is fun.

▶ Das **gerund** steht häufig als Objekt nach Verben, die Vorliebe oder Abneigung ausdrücken, wie **to enjoy, to love, to like, to hate, can't stand,** z.B. Sylvia loves **swimming**.

▶ Weitere Verben, nach denen das **gerund** verwendet wird, sind: **to finish, to imagine** (sich vorstellen), **to keep** (weiter tun), **(not) to mind** ((nicht) kümmern, (nichts) ausmachen), **to miss** (vermissen, verpassen), **to risk, to start, to stop**.

▶ Das **gerund** steht außerdem nach Verben/Adjektiven + Präpositionen, z.B. **to care about** (sich kümmern/sorgen um), **to think of** (denken an), **to feel like** (sich fühlen (wie)), **to worry about**; t**o be afraid of** (Angst haben vor), **to be bad at** (nicht gut sein), **to be famous for** (berühmt sein für), **to be tired of** (es satt haben), **to be worried about** (Angst haben um).

G **Die Verlaufsformen des Passivs** The progressive forms of the passive

Neben den dir bekannten *simple forms* des Passivs gibt es zwei *progressive forms*:

Present progressive	am / is / are + being + past participle	Many other things **are being planned**.
Past progressive	was / were + being + past participle	Many people came to look at the Skywalk while it **was being built**.

▶ Das *present progressive passive* beschreibt Vorgänge, die im Moment gerade ablaufen und noch nicht abgeschlossen sind.

▶ Das *past progressive passive* beschreibt Vorgänge, die in der Vergangenheit gerade passierten und noch nicht abgeschlossen waren.

▶ Häufig stehen die *progressive forms* nach Zeitangaben, die die Dauer einer Handlung andeuten, wie *at the moment*, *just*, *while*, *during the 1850s* etc.

G **Gerund oder Infinitiv nach bestimmten Verben**
Gerund or infinitive after certain verbs

a) Ohne Bedeutungsunterschied: *gerund = infinitive*

▶ Nach den Verben *to begin* und *to start* sowie *to like*, *to love*, *to hate* und *to prefer* kann sowohl Gerund als auch Infinitiv ohne Bedeutungsunterschied folgen, z. B.

… **prefers working** in a team (… zieht es vor …), … **prefers to do things** … (… zieht es vor…).

b) Mit Bedeutungsunterschied: *gerund ≠ infinitive*

To stop, to go on + gerund ≠	To stop, to go on + infinitive
When the instructor came in, everybody **stopped talking**. … hörte … auf zu sprechen …	After Ivy had been walking for an hour, she **stopped to have** a drink. … blieb … stehen, um etwas zu trinken.
Cody **went on practicing** until he was able to do it. … versuchte es immer wieder …	First we were told about the safety rules and then we **went on to learn** how to use a compass. … dann machten wir weiter und lernten …

▶ Das Gerund nach *stop/go on* beschreibt die Handlung, die abgebrochen / fortgeführt wird.

▶ Der Infinitiv nach *stop* und *go on* drückt die Absicht aus, etwas Neues zu tun.

To forget, to remember + gerund ≠	To forget, to remember + infinitive
I'll never **forget seeing** that terrible accident last week. Ich werde nie vergessen, wie ich … gesehen habe.	Don't **forget to wear** your helmet when you go climbing. Vergiss nicht … zu tragen …
Can you still **remember climbing** your first mountain? Kannst du dich noch daran erinnern, wie du … bestiegen hast?	Please **remember to tell** Ivy to bring her compass. … denk daran, … zu sagen …

▶ Das Gerund nach *forget* und *remember* steht für eine Handlung, die schon stattgefunden hat und an die man sich erinnert.

▶ Der Infinitiv nach *forget* und *remember* bezeichnet eine Handlung, die noch bevorsteht.

To mean + gerund ≠	To mean + infinitive
We want to get to the top by lunchtime. That **means getting up** at 5 o'clock. Das bedeutet, dass wir … aufstehen müssen.	I really **meant to bring** a compass, but I forgot. Ich hatte wirklich die Absicht, … zu bringen, …

▶ *To mean* + Gerund übersetzt man mit: **bedeuten**.

▶ *To mean* + Infinitiv drückt eine Absicht aus. Man übersetzt es oft mit: **wollen**, **beabsichtigen**.

To try + gerund ≠	To try + infinitive
If you find this difficult on your own, **try working** together with a partner. … probier's mal damit …	We **tried to get** across the river, but the water was too deep. Wir haben versucht …

▶ *To try* + Gerund drückt aus, dass eine bestimmte Methode ausprobiert wird, um ein Ziel zu erreichen.

▶ *To try* + Infinitiv drückt aus, dass versucht wird, etwas zu tun.

G Nicht-notwendige Relativsätze   Non-defining relative clauses

Defining relative clause	Non-defining relative clause
Levi Strauss was one of the immigrants **who found success in America**.	Levi Strauss, **who was born in Germany**, sold his first jeans in San Francisco in 1853.
After Alaska, California is the US state **that has most national parks**.	For a long time California, **which is about as big as Germany**, has been a magnet for legal and illegal immigrants.

▶ Notwendige Relativsätze bestimmen ihr Bezugswort (*one of the immigrants*, *the US state*) näher.
▶ Sie legen fest, wer oder was gemeint ist. Ohne sie wäre der Hauptsatz unvollständig.
▶ Zwischen Hauptsatz und notwendigem Relativsatz steht **kein Komma**.

▶ Nicht-notwendige Relativsätze enthalten zusätzliche Informationen. Der Hauptsatz wäre auch ohne diese Informationen verständlich (*Levi Strauss, California* sind durch ihre Namen definiert).
▶ Zwischen Hauptsatz und nicht-notwendigem Relativsatz stehen **Kommas**.

Relativpronomen in nicht-notwendigen Relativsätzen
Relative pronouns in non-defining relative clauses

People (who, whose)	Things (which, whose)
Illegal immigrants, **who come from Mexico**, often cross the border at night.	Hollywood, **which was founded** in 1887, is the center of the American movie industry.
Many Hispanic immigrants, **whose dream is to get rich quickly in America**, have to do the hard jobs.	Los Angeles, **whose population is still growing fast**, has become the second largest US city.

▶ In nicht-notwendigen Relativsätzen steht immer ein Relativpronomen.
▶ Für Personen verwendet man *who*.
▶ Für Dinge verwendet man *which*.
▶ *Whose* kann für Personen **und** Dinge verwendet werden und bezeichnet eine Zugehörigkeit (… Einwanderer, **deren** Traum es ist … / Los Angeles, **dessen** Bevölkerung …).

Portfolio Unit 1–2

Die Arbeit mit dem Portfolio kennst du ja bereits aus den ersten drei *Green Line* Bänden. Auch in *Green Line* 4 hast du wieder die Gelegenheit, dich selbst einzuschätzen. Blättere die ersten beiden Units in deinem Buch noch einmal durch und sieh dir die *Check-out* Seiten im Schülerbuch und auch die *Revision* Seiten im *Workbook* an. Kennzeichne dann in der Tabelle unten, was du schon gut kannst und was du noch üben solltest. In einer zusätzlichen Spalte bekommst du Tipps, wo du ggf. noch einmal nachlesen und üben kannst.

ICH KANN ...

	Kann ich schon: ✔ Muss ich noch üben: ❗	Üben im ... Seite / Übung
1 Mich auf Englisch verständigen		
... über New York sprechen		SB 12/1; 13/3; WB 4/1
... darüber sprechen, welche Informationen hilfreich sind, wenn man eine fremde Stadt besucht und den Tagesablauf planen möchte		SB 12/2b; WB 7,10
... jemanden auf mich aufmerksam machen		SB 15/6; WB 6/6
... meine Gefühle ausdrücken und über Gefühle sprechen		SB 17/1-4; WB 8/11-14
... amerikanisches Englisch von britischem unterscheiden		SB 21/1-4; WB 11/21-23
... über Einwanderung sprechen		SB 24/3
... meine Meinung in einem Text darstellen		SB 40/1-3; WB 25/10-12
... über amerikanische High Schools sprechen		SB 32/1-3; 34/3 WB 20/2b; 21/2b
... über Jobs für Jugendliche reden		SB 37/1; WB 29/5
... das *present perfect progressive* mit *since* und *for* verwenden		SB 14/2; 15/4, 5; WB 5/4, 5
... das *past perfect progressive* mit *since* und *for* verwenden		SB 16/7, 8; WB 6/7, 8
... Verben mit Objekt und Adjektiv verwenden		SB 18/2; WB 9/15
... Gradadverbien in Sätzen richtig verwenden		SB 19/4; WB 9/17
... vergangene Ereignisse kommentieren		SB 38/4, 5; WB 23/6
... sagen, was getan werden soll		SB 39/7, 8; WB 23/6
2 Lern- und Arbeitstechniken		
... Umgangssprache verstehen		SB 21/1-4; WB 11/21-23
... verstehen, was Menschen in echten Gesprächen sagen		SB 12/2; WB 4/2
... eine *KFL* Tabelle erstellen		SB 28/Step 1; WB 74/1

ICH KANN …

	Kann ich schon: ✔ Muss ich noch üben: ❗	Üben im … Seite/Übung
2 Lern- und Arbeitstechniken		
… an einer Diskussion teilnehmen	☐	SB 36/1-3; WB 22/3-5
… meine Meinung in einem *pro and con text* ausdrücken	☐	SB 40/1-3; WB 25/10-12
3 Sonst kann ich auch …		
… einen Touristenführer verstehen	☐	SB 12/2; WB 4/2
… in der Gruppe über bestimmte Themen diskutieren	☐	SB 13/3; WB 74/1-3
… Notizen zu den wichtigsten Informationen einer Radiosendung machen	☐	SB 20/9
… einem Lesetext bestimmte Informationen entnehmen	☐	SB 24/2; 30/1; WB 18/1
… eine Biografie schreiben	☐	SB 31/3; WB 19/3
… eine Werbung gestalten	☐	SB 31/4; WB 74/2
… Informationen zielgerichtet aus der einen in die andere Sprache übertragen	☐	SB 31/6; WB 19/5; 24/9
… *Linking words* einsetzen, um einen Text klarer zu strukturieren	☐	SB 41/1; WB 26/13
… *compounds* bilden	☐	SB 41/3
… einen englischen Song verstehen	☐	SB 41/5
4 In der letzten Klassenarbeit konnte ich gut / hatte ich Probleme mit …		
	☐	
	☐	
	☐	
	☐	
	☐	

5 Am liebsten mache ich …

_____

_____

_____

_____

_____

Portfolio   Unit 3–5

Gratuliere! Du hast den vierten *Green Line* Band erfolgreich durchgearbeitet. Kreuze auch für die letzten drei Units an, wie du dich selbst einschätzt.

ICH KANN ...

	Kann ich schon: ✔ Muss ich noch üben: !	Üben im ... Seite/Übung
1 Mich auf Englisch verständigen		
... anhand von Bildern über den *American West* sprechen	☐	SB 46/1; WB 30/1
... über *mobility* sprechen	☐	SB 47/3, 4; WB 30/3
... mich in *Small talk* Situationen höflich unterhalten	☐	SB 51/1-4; WB 34/11, 12
... über die Geschichte des *Ameriacan West* sprechen	☐	SB 52/1; WB 35-36
... über Klischees sprechen	☐	SB 58/3
... mich positiver ausdrücken	☐	SB 59/4; WB 39/22
... die wichtigsten Fakten aus einem englischen Text auf Deutsch wiedergeben	☐	SB 65/6; WB 32/3; 63/15
... über Abenteuer sprechen	☐	SB 67/5; 69/5; WB 46/3b; 47/3b
... Wünsche und Erwartungen äußern	☐	SB 71/2; WB 49/6
... über Erfahrungen mit dem Lernen sprechen	☐	SB 73/9
... Ängste ausdrücken und anderen dabei helfen, mit ihren Ängsten umzugehen	☐	SB 72/6; WB 50/10
... über Kalifornien sprechen	☐	SB 84/1; WB 58/1
... über Immigration in Kalifornien sprechen	☐	WB 60/7
... in entsprechenden Situationen das richtige Sprachregister verwenden	☐	SB 88/1-3; WB 61/8-10
... mich zum Thema Umwelt äußern	☐	SB 91/7, 8; WB 64/17
... über Probleme des *show business* sprechen	☐	SB 92-94; WB 65
... das *gerund* richtig verwenden	☐	SB 49/2, 3, 5; WB 31/4, 5; 32/7
... das *present* und *past progressive passive* verwenden	☐	SB 52-53; WB 35-36
... den *infinitive after question words and superlatives* richtig benutzen	☐	SB 72/3, 4; WB 49/7, 8
... Verben mit *infinitive* oder *gerund* richtig verwenden	☐	SB 73/7; WB 50/11
... Relativsätze richtig verwenden	☐	SB 86/2; 87/3-5; WB 59/3-5; 60/6
... *participles* als Adjektive verwenden	☐	SB 89/2; 90/3; WB 62/12

ICH KANN ...

	Kann ich schon: ✔ Muss ich noch üben: !	Üben im ... Seite/Übung
2 Lern- und Arbeitstechniken		
... Grammatik verstehen und sie im Gedächtnis behalten	☐	SB 54/1-3; WB 37/17, 18
... verschiedene Textsorten unterscheiden	☐	SB 74/2; WB 51/12
... mithilfe eines Plans einen eigenen Text verfassen	☐	SB 74/1-4; WB 51/12, 13
... ein *word web* zu einem bestimmten Thema erstellen und mithilfe dessen einen Text entwickeln	☐	SB 65/4
... eine Geschichte schreiben	☐	SB 58/4; WB 66/21-24
3 Sonst kann ich auch ...		
... einer echten Diskussion folgen und Fragen dazu beantworten	☐	SB 47/3; WB 30/3
... die Personenkonstellation in einem längeren Text analysieren	☐	SB 58/2; WB 47/2
... einen englischen Song verstehen und analysieren	☐	SB 62-63
... über den Stil eines Textes sprechen	☐	SB 67/3; WB 75/2
... eine *movie review* lesen	☐	SB 70/1-3; WB 48/5; 56/1
... zwischen *facts* und *opinion* unterscheiden	☐	SB 70/3; WB 48/5
... anhand einer Ausgangssituation auf einem Foto einen Text verfassen	☐	SB 81/4; WB 55/4
4 In der letzten Klassenarbeit konnte ich gut/hatte ich Probleme mit ...		
	☐	
	☐	
	☐	
	☐	
	☐	

5 Am liebsten mache ich ...

_____

_____

_____

_____

_____

2 Listening: I was there – at Wounded Knee

Philip Wells was part Sioux and part white and was working for the US army because he could speak both the Sioux language and English.
Listen to Philip Wells's report about the Battle at Wounded Knee and tick ✔ *the right answer.*

	right	wrong	not in the text
1. Big Foot told Colonel Forsyth that his men's guns were broken.	☐	☐	☐
2. The medicine man was dancing the Ghost Dance.	☐	☐	☐
3. The fight started because one of the soldiers shot the medicine man.	☐	☐	☐
4. Philip Wells did not like the Indians.	☐	☐	☐
5. The medicine man hated doctors.	☐	☐	☐
6. Philip Wells shot the medicine man.	☐	☐	☐

3 Speaking: Talking about a photo

a) *Describe what you can see in the picture. Then talk about the people in it. How do they feel? Why are they celebrating?*

b) *How do you celebrate events like these in your culture?*

4 Writing texts: A pro and con text

`+++Should Native Americans be allowed to build tourist attractions like the Skywalk on their land?+++`

Write a pro and con text about this topic (10–15 lines). Look at p. 40 in your book for tips and help. Use your exercise book.

5 Mediation: Bury[12] my heart at Wounded Knee, 2007

*You are on a school exchange in the US. One of your German friends has found a DVD called **Bury my heart at Wounded Knee**. His English is not good enough to understand the text. Tell him the most important things about the movie in German.*

The movie tells the story of three people: Charles Eastman, a young Sioux doctor, Sitting Bull[13], the famous Sioux chief, and Senator Hugh Dawes[14], a member of the US government. Eastman tries to improve the situation of the Sioux on the reservation and the Senator tries to get President Grant to help the Indians, too.
The Indians dance the Ghost Dance and hope for a better future, but when Sitting Bull is killed and many Indians die at Wounded Knee, these hopes die with them.

[12]**to bury** ['beri] = begraben • [13]**bull** [bʊl] = Bulle • [14]**Senator Hugh Dawes** ['senətə hjuː ˌdɔːz]

> Do the exercises on this page *(Choice A)* or the exercises on the next page *(Choice B).*

Unit 4   Extreme action

1 **Find the words** *(Choice A)*   (→ PB p. 67)

a) *Complete these sentences about the beginning of Ralston's story.*

On April 25, 2003, Aron Ralston from Aspen, C O L O R A D O ,

drove to a national park in ___ ___ ___ |__| . That night he ___ ___ |__| ___ ___

in his |__| ___ ___ ___ - up and the next morning he cycled to the top of Blue John Canyon. After

that he continued on ___ ___ |__| ___ , but while he was ___ |__| ___ ___ ___ ___ ___ ___

down into the canyon between two |__| ___ ___ ___ ___ ___ , a big

___ ___ ___ ___ ___ |__| ___ fell and landed on his ___ ___ |__| ___ .

b) *Use the letters in the boxes to find something that might have helped Ralston when his accident happened.* |__| |__| |_L_| |__| |__| |__| |__| |__| |__|

2 **Put the notes in the right order** *(Choice A)*   (→ PB p. 67)

Match the six days of Aron Ralston's ordeal to the six sentences.

Sat. April 26	still no success with ropes
Sun. April 27	broke arm and cut himself free
Mon. April 28	hand trapped by boulder
Tues. April 29	realized would have to lose hand
Wed. April 30	tried using ropes to lift boulder
Thurs. May 1	no more water to drink

3 **A press conference** *(Choice A)*   (→ PB p. 67)

a) *How do you think Aron Ralston would answer these questions at a press conference?*
Use your exercise book.

1. "What was your first reaction when your hand was trapped?"
2. "Why did you finally decide that you had to cut off your own hand?"
3. "What kind of climbing experience did you already have before your trip to Utah?"
4. "When and why did you first get interested in climbing?"
5. "The pain must have been really terrible when you broke your arm and cut yourself free.
Can you tell us how you were able to deal with that?"

b) *Your turn: Have you heard or read reports about other people in extreme situations?*
Work in groups and tell each other what happened.

1 Find the mistakes in these pictures of *Downriver (Choice B)*　(→ PB p. 69)

There are two mistakes in each picture. Explain them in your exercise book.

A Before Granite Falls …　　**B** Hermit Rapids …　　**C** Crystal Rapids …

2 Put in the correct names *(Choice B)*　(→ PB p. 69)

1. _____ can be reckless and wants to be number one in the group.

2. _____ is quite brave, but is silly to try and run Crystal Rapids with Troy.

3. _____ realizes most of them have not been thinking for themselves.

4. _____ says she wants to stay with the others for as long as possible.

5. _____ and _____ also just follow what other people say or do.

6. The only member of the group who is strong enough to stand up to Troy is _____ .

Troy　Pug　Freddy　Jessie　Star　Rita　Adam

3 Complete the sentences *(Choice B)*　(→ PB p. 69)

a) *Give the information in your own words.*

1. The rapids at Granite Falls were nasty, but both boats

   got to the bottom safely. _____

> **TIP**
> You'll find it easier to use your own words if you just try to remember the story and don't look at your book.

2. The helicopters that were chasing them gave up when _____

3. The noise they could hear from Crystal Rapids was very loud because _____

   _____

4. Troy and Adam decided to run Crystal Rapids in one boat. The other kids _____

   _____

5. When there was no sign of Troy or Adam, the others _____

b) *Your turn: Tell your group about another exciting book you have read (in English or in German). Say what happens in the story.*

READING SKILLS

4   **Complete these definitions of typical movie review words**   (→ PB p. 70)

1.   screenplay: This _is the script with all the words and actions in the movie._

2.   plot: This explains _____

3.   rating: This is an opinion about how _____

4.   score: This is another word for _____

5.   running time: This tells you _____

6.   cast: This is a list of _____

5   **Read this DVD review**   (→ PB p. 70)

Emile Hirsch
Marcia Gay Harden
William Hurt
Jena Malone
Catherine Keener
Brian Dierker
Vince Vaughn
Zach Galifianakis
Kristen Stewart
and Hal Holbrook

INTO THE WILD
screenplay and directed by Sean Penn

142

FAIRBANKS CITY TRANSIT SYSTEM

INTO THE WILD

2007
Director: Sean Penn
Screenplay: Sean Penn
(based on book of same name by John Krakauer)

Rating: ★ ★ ★ ★ ★
Songs: All songs by Eddie Vedder ('Pearl Jam' frontman)

This is the true story of East Coast rich-kid Christopher McCandless (Actor Emile Hirsch in the starring role does a great job and he looks so much like the real McCandless that it is weird!), fresh out of college in his early 20s, who has had enough of his family and modern life and decides to travel around and disappear. We follow him on his survival trip into the Alaskan wilderness.

The bad news first: This is a very sad story. And it is a true story, and that makes it even sadder. And, it is a very long movie: three hours!

The good news: Although sad and long, this movie is excellent and gets a five-star-rating.

To cut a long story short, this movie does two things extremely well: Giving viewers McCandless' feeling of absolute freedom, while also showing how dangerous nature can be. Yes, I can recommend this movie to anyone – in my opinion it is the best Hollywood movie in 2007.

a) *Use different colors to underline this information in the review:*

1. title of the movie (black)
2. actors in main roles (pink)
3. setting[1] (grey)
4. plot and main action (blue)
5. positive comments (green)
6. negative comments (red)

b) *Write two or three sentences to explain the difference between the two main parts of the review. (The work you did in a) can help you.)*

The first part gives some basic information about _____

_____

_____

c) *Say who you think might enjoy watching* Into the wild. *What about you?*

[1] **setting** ['setɪŋ] = Handlungsort

6 Write about different people's wishes or expectations (→ PB p. 71; Grammar → PB G14)

*A girl from New York has decided to do a rock-climbing course in a canyon in Utah next month.
Read what different people say to her and find the right ideas to complete the sentences.*

- "You should go to the gym."
- "Please tell me about it."
- "You can send photos to my cell phone!"

- "You don't have to call every day." ✔
- "Don't forget me!"
- "I wish you'd do a different activity."

1. Her mother hopes she will phone home, but *does not expect* ___her to call every day.___

2. Her brother wants to see the canyon and *would like* ___her_____

3. Her best friend thinks she should get fit before the course. She *advises* _____

4. Her grandfather is very interested in the course and *wants* _____

5. Her father thinks it sounds dangerous and *would prefer* _____

6. Her boyfriend is worried she might meet another guy. He *does not want* _____

7 Sentences with question words and infinitives (→ PB p. 72; Grammar → PB G14)

a) *Look at the photo and imagine the questions that went through the person's
head before his / her bungee jump. Start with the ideas below and write at
least four sentences in your exercise book.*

Example: He wasn't sure when to jump out of the helicopter.

He +	didn't know wasn't sure had no idea wondered	+	when how whether what where	+ to +	do with his arms. deal with his fear. look during the jump. jump out of the helicopter. laugh or scream.

b) *Imagine you are in a scary situation. Tell the others what questions are going through your head.
The others have to guess the situation.*

8 Match the words in A and B to complete the text (→ PB p. 72; Grammar → PB G14)

A the first problem • the only thing • the worst place • the best person ✔ • the last

B to have • to go • to deal with • to do • to cross

"Ed is a nice guy, but on Sunday Rob and I discovered he isn't ___the best person___

_____ hiking with! Ed had the map, and _____ _____ was how to

find the trail again after we had gotten lost. Rob and I managed to get across a little river, but Ed was

_____ _____ and he slipped and hurt his leg. It was _____

_____ an accident – we were miles from anywhere and without a phone. In the end

_____ _____ was to carry Ed all the way back."

👥 **9** Partner activity: A talk with an instructor

One partner is A and the other one is B. Look at the German sentences and create an English dialogue between a boy (A) and an instructor (B) on an abseiling course. The words in brackets¹ can help you to check what your partner says, but other answers are also possible. When you have finished, change roles.

A

Du erklärst dem Lehrer, dass du es nicht tun kannst. Du hast zu viel Angst.
(You aren't the only one to feel scared. It's normal.)
Du antwortest, dass du aber keine Ahnung hast, was man mit den Seilen machen muss.
(That's why I'm here – to teach you how to use them.)
Du sagst, dass du einverstanden bist und dass du es versuchen möchtest. Du fragst, was du jetzt tun musst.
(Nothing at all yet. I just want you to stay calm.)
Sage, dass es nicht leicht ist, ruhig zu bleiben, wenn man stürzen könnte.
(I promise you, it isn't possible to fall!)

B

Du versprichst ihm, dass es nicht möglich ist zu stürzen.
(It isn't easy to stay calm when you might fall.)
Du willst bloß, dass er ruhig bleibt. Sage ihm, dass er noch gar nichts tun muss.
(OK, I'd like to try it. What do I have to do?)
Du antwortest, dass du deshalb da bist – um ihm beizubringen, wie man sie verwendet.
(But I have no idea what to do with the ropes.)
Du sagst dem Jungen, dass er nicht der Einzige ist, der Angst hat. Das ist normal.
(I can't do it. I'm too scared.)

10 How to: Help someone deal with their fears (→ PB p. 72)

Use your own ideas to complete what A says, and then think of good answers for B. (The Useful phrases on page 72 in your book can help you.) Write the dialogues down. Use your exercise book.

A: The test for my driver's licence is tomorrow. It would be awful if …

B: … **1**

A: I wish I hadn't agreed to take part in that radio quiz. When I think about it, I feel …

B: … **2**

A: I hate the idea of moving and having to go to a new school. I'm worried that …

B: … **3**

A: I think there might be a serious problem with my grades, but I'm too scared to …

B: … **4**

11 Complete this opinion with the correct verbs (→ PB p. 73; Grammar → PB G15)

Think about the meaning of the verbs in blue. Which form should follow: infinitive or gerund? Use the verbs on the right.

 read   put on   do   risk

I don't like activities that **mean** _____ accidents. I know skiing is dangerous because

one of my friends seriously hurt his leg. But he still **continues** _____ it. I **remember**

_____ an article once about how many people seriously hurt their heads on the slopes.

Not me! I never **forget** _____ a helmet when I go skiing.

¹**bracket** ['brækɪt] = Klammer

WRITING TEXTS

12 **Look at different types of texts** (→ PB p. 74)

Read parts of different texts. Write down what types of texts they are.

> She walked with slow, heavy steps to the door and then looked back sadly over her shoulder. "I'm sorry," she said. "I didn't mean it to be like this."

> MICROMAGIC – tasty meals you can make in only minutes! Now with less sugar than before, so they're even healthier.

> *Mel: (to Dan)* What exciting news!
> *Dan:* Yes, but don't forget it's a secret.
> *(Dan leaves stage. After a short pause, Mel phones someone.)*
> *Mel:* Hi! You'll never believe this!

1. _story_

2. _____

3. _____

> The characters are interesting, the plot is exciting and the style makes it easy to read. This is one you won't want to put down until you get to the last page.

> Five people were rescued from the roof of a skyscraper in downtown Chicago yesterday. The emergency began with a fire on the tenth story of the building.

> It was great to hear from you. Sorry, I didn't reply right away, but I had a lot of work to do for school. It seems ages since our adventure course in the Rockies.

4. _____

5. _____

6. _____

13 **Write about an American teenager** (→ PB p. 74)

a) *Use your own ideas to fill in this personal profile.*

Name: _____ **Age:** ____

From: _____

Family background: _____

_____

Character: _____

_____

Hobbies: _____

Any other information: _____

_____

- city / state?
- parents' jobs?
- live with both parents?
- brother or sister?
- what kind of person? (quiet / funny / friendly / …)
- good at sport?
- music fan?
- problems at home / school?
- dreams for the future?

> **TIP**
>
> **Improve your style**
> - Link the ideas to make longer sentences.
> - Try to start each sentence differently.

b) *Turn the personal profile you created in a) into a paragraph with information about the teenager. Use your exercise book.*

c) *Check your partner's text. Make helpful suggestions about what could be improved.*

14 Work with verbs and nouns that go together

Put in the correct verbs and nouns. (Be careful with the tense and form of the verbs!)

VERBS:	**NOUNS:**
make • take ✓ • solve • learn • give	an opinion • a mistake • a risk • a problem • a skill

1. He is a reckless person, so he often ___takes___ when other people would be scared.

2. It would be better if you _____ , so we know what you think about the idea.

3. If you go on the course, you _____ and have fun at the same time.

4. We went the wrong way because I _____ when I was using the compass.

5. When you are trying _____ , the first thing to do is to stop and think!

15 Where is the stress?

Say the words and then underline the parts that are stressed.

re<u>view</u> • structure • element • instructor • confidence • reaction • adrenaline • realize

16 Guess the meaning of phrases with 'take'

a) *Draw lines between the pairs of speakers. The context can help you to guess the right phrases.*

1. "Is it really true?"　　　　　　　　　　"It's a terrible noise! I can't take it anymore."

2. "He doesn't listen to what I say."　　　"I know. He never takes any notice of anyone."

3. "Tell me something about the plot."　　"Well, the invitation is there. Take it or leave it."

4. "What's wrong with my music?"　　　　"You can take my word for it!"

5. "Hm. I can't decide if I want to go with you."　"Let's take a look. I'm quite good with bikes."

6. "There's something wrong with my brakes."　"Well, the story takes place in Alaska."

b) *What would you say in German for the phrases with 'take'? Use your exercise book.*

17 Word pairs　(→ PB p. 75)

Use the words below to make five pairs of words with the same meaning and five pairs of words with opposite meaning. Who is fastest? Use your exercise book.

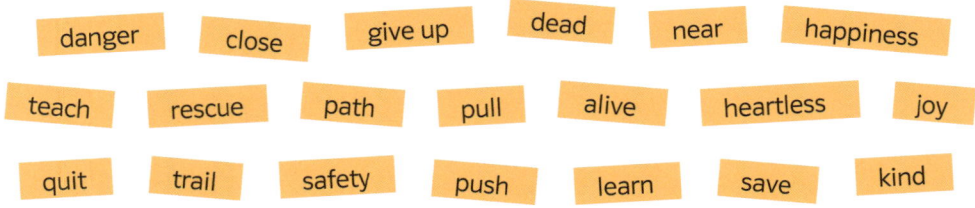

danger • close • give up • dead • near • happiness • teach • rescue • path • pull • alive • heartless • joy • quit • trail • safety • push • learn • save • kind

18 Read this for fun

The kid looked up at the scary cliff which his instructor wanted him to climb. "Do people often fall from the top?" he asked nervously. "No," the instructor replied, "once is usually enough."

19 Complete the sentences with an object and infinitive (→ PB p. 76; Grammar → PB G14)

1. The hiker wants _the rain_ _____

2. The boy would like _____

3. The boy wants the spider _____

4. The kids would prefer the water _____

5. The instructor expects the girl _____

20 Put in the correct form of the verbs: infinitive or gerund (→ PB p. 76; Grammar → PB G15)

1. "Sorry, I didn't mean _____ (burn) the fish." – "I know, but you should try

_____ (concentrate) when you're cooking!"   2. "The guy I was with today never stopped

_____ (talk) about himself." – "Well, remember _____ (ask) if you can have

a different partner tomorrow."   3. "I'm sure you'll never forget _____ (meet) that bear!"

– "You're right! I'll go on _____ (have) bad dreams about it for years!"

4. "Have you ever stopped _____ (think) where this river comes from?" – "Finding out

where it starts would mean _____ (climb) high up into the mountains."

21 Explain what information you need

*You are phoning an outdoor adventure center in Colorado.
Turn the questions into infinitive constructions.*

> **TIP**
> Explaining what you want to know
> often sounds more polite than asking
> questions.

1. How can I book a course? → I'm calling to find out _how to book a course._ _____

2. Should I do the easy course? → I need advice about _whether_ _____

3. What clothes should I bring? → It would help if you could suggest _____

4. How do I get to the center? → I'm not exactly sure _____

5. Should I fly to Denver or Aspen? → I don't know _____

6. When do I have to pay for the course? → I'd like to know _____

⟨Revision for tests⟩ Standards

1 Understanding the text: The hardest sled[1] dog race in the world

a) *Read the text. There are six sentences missing in the text. Choose the correct sentence for each gap from the list below and write the letters (A-F) next to the correct sentences.*

1. ____ No more than 50 teams are allowed and the team drivers must be at least 18 years old.

2. ____ It sometimes takes 16 days until the final dog team finishes.

3. ____ The race gets its name from the Yukon River.

4. ____ There are ten checkpoints along the trail.

5. ____ The Yukon Quest Champion wins $35,000.

6. ____ Even for those who just want to watch, the race is a real challenge and an adventure.

In the wild landscape of the Yukon[2] and Alaska, the Yukon Quest[3] International Sled Dog Race runs every year in February and has done so since 1984. **A** When the river is frozen
5 in the winter it is called 'the highway of the north' because it is the easiest way to travel – although no travel here is easy. The Yukon Quest Trail follows old gold rush and mail[4] delivery dog
10 sled 'highways' to the Klondike[5] and Alaska. The 1,000 miles (1,600 km) between Whitehorse and Fairbanks are sometimes difficult and dangerous. The weather can be the coldest of the year and it is not predictable.
15 Sled dog teams with 14 dogs and their dog team driver run for two weeks across one of the last wild landscapes in North America. **B** They can only get help in Dawson[6] City, the home of the 1898 Klondike Gold Rush and the half-way point
20 of the race, so all the equipment and food they need must be carried on the sled.

  The $200,000 prize money is shared between the first 15 finishing teams, but all the teams that complete the race get $1,000. **C** Sonny Lindner
25 became the first Yukon Quest champion when he completed the race in just over 12 days. **D** **E** Some checkpoints are more than 200 miles from the next one, so the teams are really on their own. There is regular race news with

Alaska — *Yukon Territory*

Circle
Central
Steese MP 101
Angel Creek
Northpole
Fairbanks
Biederman's
Eagle
Dawson City

The Yukon Quest

Steward River
Pelly Crossing
McCabe Creek
Carmacks
Braeburn
Whitehorse

information on dog teams' positions and times. 30 Race vets check the dogs regularly to make sure that they are fit to continue.

  The trail runs[7] across frozen rivers, climbs over four mountain areas, and passes[8] through lonely villages. With temperatures below 40°C, 35 100 mile-an-hour winds, open water and weak ice all working against the teams, the Yukon Quest is a true test for both the team drivers and their dogs. **F**

b) *Would you like to take part in a race like this? Say why / why not.*

¹**sled** [sled] = Schlitten • ²**Yukon** [ˈjuːkɑːn] • ³**quest** [kwest] = Herausforderung, Abenteuer • ⁴**mail** [meɪl] = Post •
⁵**Klondike** [ˈklɑːndaɪk] • ⁶**Dawson** [ˈdɑːsn] • ⁷**to run** [rʌn] = *hier*: führen • ⁸**to pass** [pɑːs] = vorbeiführen

2 Listening: Bungee jumping

Listen to a radio programme about dangerous sports. Take notes about what you can remember.

1. What was the 'Dangerous Sports Club'? _____

   _____

2. What must be checked before a jump? _____

3. Why does Frank like the sport? _____

3 Speaking: Sport on TV

`+++There is too much sport on TV.+++`

*Discuss with your partner. Do you agree / disagree?
Say why.*

4 Writing texts: A diary

*Look at the picture and write the girl's diary for the day
shown in the picture.*

5 Mediation: Stacy Peralta

*Your English friend finds this report in your school magazine.
He is interested in skateboarding and asks you to tell him the most
important things about Stacy Peralta in English.*

Stacy Peralta wurde 1957 in einer ärmlichen Gegend in Kalifornien geboren. Er vertrieb sich die Zeit damit, am Strand mit seinen Freunden zu surfen. Das *Zephyr⁹ Surf Team*, eine Gruppe radikaler Surfer, machte Stacy und seinen Freunden oft den Platz streitig, sodass sie versuchten an Land zu „surfen". Aus diesen Versuchen entwickelte sich schnell ein Trend, von dem auch das *Zephyr Surf Team* rasch Notiz nahm. Sie erlernten ebenfalls die Technik an Land zu surfen, und gründeten das *Zephyr Skate Team*, dem Peralta auch bald angehörte. Nach und nach entwickelten sie immer mehr Techniken und gingen damit auch an die Öffentlichkeit. Etliche Teammitglieder wurden von der Industrie zur Vermarktung ihrer Ideen unter Vertrag genommen und das *Zephyr Skate Team* löste sich nach und nach auf. Nach zahlreichen Erfolgen als Skateboarder und als Entwickler von Skateboard Designs gründete Peralta zusammen mit George Powell die Skateboardfirma *Powell & Peralta*.

Die vielen Demovideos, die Peralta für Firmen produzierte, waren nicht nur einflussreich, sondern machten ihn auch zu einem berühmten Regisseur, der sein Publikum mit interessanten Dokumentarfilmen zum Thema Skateboard begeistert.

⁹**Zephyr** [ˈzefə]

〈Revision for tests〉 Standards

1 Understanding the text: Two movie reviews

The River Wild, Running time: 108 minutes, USA (1994),
★ ★ ★ ☆

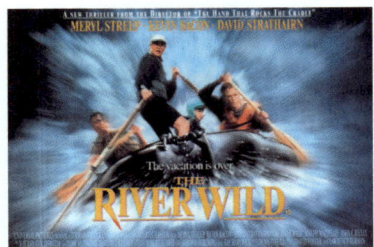

Meryl Streep[1] plays the role of Gail[2] in this Curtis Hanson action movie. She was once a rafting[3] guide in Montana, but is now taking her son and Maggie, their dog, on a rafting trip there during summer vacation.

The husband, Tom, played by David Strathairn[3], does not want to come at first, but he surprises his family and they start what is going to be a different river adventure from the one they expected. Three men follow them down the river. Tom does not know that the men are killers who are being chased by the police. When one of them, Wade[4] (Kevin Bacon), falls into the river, Tom saves him. Gail and Tom work together in their battle with the river and the killers.

Movies like this are so predictable, but Streep and Bacon do a great job. Of course, you will also love the rafting scenes and will want to book your next rafting vacation on one of the wild Montana rivers. But take the family to see *The River Wild first*.

Bagdad Café, Running time: 92 minutes, Germany / USA (1987), ★ ★ ★ ☆

When Jasmin[5] (Marianne Sägebrecht), a German tourist, walks away from her husband after a fight in the middle of the Mojave Desert and arrives at Brenda's café-motel[6], it is the start of a sometimes difficult, but very funny friendship.

Brenda, a free-thinking black woman, has just thrown her husband out of the Bagdad Café. She is left with her children, an Italian cook, a tattoo artist, and Rudi Cox, a painter, who once worked in Hollywood. Crazy? Yes, this movie has got everything a dark comedy needs. Jasmin starts to clean the place and soon the café is a real success story. It becomes a fun place for all the people in the Bagdad community, but is everyone happy?

Director Percy Adlon[7] has done a wonderful job. This movie says a lot about Europe and America and the American Dream. It has won a number of awards and it will win you over, too, when you laugh about the situations the characters get into.

a) *Read the movie reviews and then fill in the gaps.*

1. Curtis Hanson is the __d_____ of the action movie.

2. Tom saves Wade in the movie, but he does not know that he is a __k_____ .

3. Meryl Streep and Kevin Bacon do a very good __i_____ in *The River Wild*.

4. A lot of action movies are very __p_____ . There are not many real surprises.

5. The __r_____ of the film *Bagdad Café* is 92 minutes.

6. The opening scene in *Bagdad Café* is set in the __M_____ .

7. *Bagdad Café* is not an action movie, it is a dark __c_____ .

8. The movie *Bagdad Café* is so good that it has won a lot of __a_____ .

b) *Which of the movies is more interesting? Why?*

[1]**Meryl Streep** [ˌmerl ˈstriːp] • [2]**Gail** [geɪl] • [3]**Strathairn** [strɑːˈθɜːrn] • [4]**Wade** [weɪd] • [5]**Jasmin** [ˈdʒæzmɪn] • [6]**motel** [məʊˈtel] = Motel • [7]**Percy Adlon** [ˌpɜːsi ˈædlən]

2 Listening: A film director speaks

The director of Bagdad Café, *Percy Adlon, is talking to some American film students.*

a) *Write down three important topics he mentions in his talk.*

_____

b) *Right, wrong or not in the text?*

	right	wrong	not in the text
1. Percy Adlon has lived in the US since 1987.	☐	☐	☐
2. He wanted to live and work somewhere else. So he came to the US.	☐	☐	☐
3. His movies are not in German because more people watch movies in English.	☐	☐	☐
4. His movies deal with American subjects.	☐	☐	☐
5. Percy Adlon and his family liked the Mojave Desert.	☐	☐	☐
6. The idea for the story for *Bagdad Café* came from a café on Route 66.	☐	☐	☐

3 Speaking: A discussion about movies

Decide who is partner A and who is partner B. Partner A wants to watch Bagdad Café *and partner B wants to watch* The River Wild. *Each one takes notes about his/her favorite movie. Then start a discussion on which movie to watch together this evening.*

4 Writing: A screenplay

This is a scene from an adventure movie. Give the characters names. What has happened? What are they talking about now? Describe the situation and then write the dialogue. Use your exercise book.

5 Mediation: A magazine article

You are reading a movie magazine when a friend asks you what you are reading about. You start to read it to him, but he does not understand. Tell him the most important things about Roland Emmerich in German.

Roland Emmerich is one of the few German directors who is well-known in Hollywood. He has used a lot of computer tricks in his movies and has now become one of the big Hollywood directors. In 1992 Emmerich's *Universal Soldier*, a science fiction movie, got great reviews. Two other science fiction movies, *Independence Day* and *Godzilla*, have also been very successful. *The Day*

After Tomorrow is another one of his movies. Lots of famous stars have worked with him. Jodie Foster and Mel Gibson are just two of them. He was born on November 10, 1955, in Sindelfingen near Stuttgart. At school he was interested in art and later he was a student in Munich. It was in Munich where he learned about film and TV. Today he lives and works in America most of the time.

Unit 5   The Golden State

1 **Famous Californians**   (→ PB p. 84)

a) *Choose words from below to complete the texts. (You don`t need all of them.)*

advertising • awards • climate • earned • golf • deep • movies • near • poor •
famous • really • relatives • spent • studios • supports • worried

b) *Do you know the names of the two people? Write the correct names as the titles of the texts. Check the Internet for help.*

Name: _____

He was born in 1974 in Los Angeles. His mother's _____ came from Germany, his father's from Italy. He became a world-famous Hollywood star as the _____ boy Jack Dawson in *Titanic*. He has won many _____ , even one Golden Globe, and he _____ environmental protection.

Name: _____

His first name is _____ Eldrick, but most of his fans don't know that. He was born _____ Los Angeles in 1975, and his father taught him to play _____ very early. As a boy he won many competitions, and in 1996 he became a _____ player. Since then he has _____ millions in prize money and from _____ .

c) *Your turn: Write a text about a famous person that you like a lot and who is from Germany. Use your exercise book.*

2 **Listening: What do Californians think?**   (→ PB p. 84)

What do the three Californians like / hate about their state? Make notes in the grid.

	1. man	2. woman	3. woman
loves ...	_____ _____	_____ _____	_____ _____
hates ...	_____ _____	_____ _____	_____ _____

3 New Californians: Defining and non-defining relative clauses (→ PB p. 87; Grammar → PB G16)

a) *Draw lines to match the two halves of the sentences.*

1. Miguel is one of the thousands of illegal immigrants ☐ who cross

2. His job ☐ which a friend

3. His boss ☐ whose family have been fruit farmers for fifty

4. The fruit ☐ which Miguel picks ☐ is

5. Miguel's wife ☐ who still lives in

6. California is home to more and

usually sent to states in the northern US.

Mexico ☐ hopes to cross the border next year.

the US-Mexican border every year.

more people ☐ whose mother tongue is Spanish.

helped him to find ☐ is not paid very well.

years ☐ is one of the richest men in the region.

b) *Put in commas for the relative clauses where they are needed.*

4 Make the text more interesting (→ PB p. 87; Grammar → PB G16)

Use non-defining relative clauses to add the extra information on the right to the text. Use your exercise book.

Every year thousands of Mexicans cross the Californian border. ☐3☐ Many of them are illegal immigrants. ☐___☐ If these new Californians do not speak English, ☐___☐ their job chances are not very good. But they usually find jobs with farmers. ☐___☐ Juanita had one of these jobs, ☐___☐ but she did not work in the fields for very long. She took the advice of her cousin Ramon, ☐___☐ and now she works as a cook. She says she does not want to end her life like her parents. ☐___☐

1. They never had any success.
2. The job was boring and unhealthy.
3. The border runs from the Pacific Ocean to the Colorado River. ✔
4. Ramon had a job as a waiter in town.
5. They are the poorest of the poor.
6. The farmers need the cheap workers from Mexico.
7. English is still the most important language.

5 The 'Razzies'¹ (→ PB p. 87; Grammar → PB G16)

Complete the text with the missing defining or non-defining relative clauses from the list below. Sometimes there is more than one possible answer!

which are presented the day before the Oscars • which nobody wants •
which is between January and March each year

Awards Season ☐ _____ ☐ is an exciting

time to be in L.A.. This is the time when the world's most important awards shows take place: the

Grammys (music), the Golden Globes (film) and the Oscars (also film). But there is another popular

award ☐ _____ : a Golden Raspberry!

The Razzies ☐ _____ ☐ are awards

for the worst actors and worst films. Britney Spears and Bruce Willis were 'winners' for example.

¹**Razzies** ['ræziz] *Abkürzung für* The Golden Raspberry = Die Goldene Himbeere

6 **Chinese immigrants to California** (→ PB p. 87; Grammar → PB G16)

Turn one of the sentences into a defining or a non-defining relative clause.

1. In the 1850s many people left China and came to California. China was a poor country.

   In the 1850s many people left China, which
   _____

2. Most ships from China arrived in San Francisco. The Chinese called San Francisco 'Gold Mountain'.

   _____
   _____

3. The men usually came alone, but sometimes they brought their sons. The sons were old enough to work.

   _____
   _____

4. In the 1880s new laws stopped immigration from China. The laws were not changed until the 20th century.

   _____
   _____

7 **Tandem activity: Too many Mexican immigrants?**

Two Californians, Taylor and Ben, are discussing this question.
Taylor is worried about the situation, but Ben does not want to change anything.

Taylor

1. illegal immigrants • take our jobs
   (That's not true. Californians don't want these hard jobs.)

2. Mexicans • do anything • for money • criminal activities
   (That's not fair. Many Mexicans have a hard life, and they don't earn much money.)

3. don't have to • come here • stay • Mexico • work there
   (But wouldn't you look for a better life in another country, too?)

4. mmh • right • Mexicans • good work • for us

Ben

1. (All these illegal immigrants! They are taking our jobs away from us.)
   not true • Californians • not want • hard jobs

2. (Mexicans will do anything for money – criminal activities, too.)
   not fair • many Mexicans • hard life • not earn • much money

3. (They don't have to come here. They can stay in Mexico and work there.)
   But • would you not • look • better life • in another country?

4. (Mmh, you're right. The Mexicans do good work for us, I guess.)

TALKWISE

8 The right register for the situation (→ PB p. 88)

a) *Should you be polite or casual in these situations? Write a 'p' for polite and a 'c' for casual in the boxes.*

calling a DJ in a phone-in show ____ • buying concert tickets by phone ____ •

phoning a computer company's hotline ____ • talking to somebody in your sports team ____

b) *Add two more situations to each category.*

polite	casual
_____	_____
_____	_____

9 Complete the dialogues (→ PB p. 88)

a) *Underline the polite phrases in red and the casual phrases in blue.*

Hey, what's going on there? • <u>Excuse me, do you have any maps?</u> • Stop that noise, will you? •
Oh no! My cell phone's gone. • I'm sorry, but Sharon isn't home. • Would you like to order now?

b) *Make mini-dialogues. Write down each phrase from a) in the right category.*
Then write speaker B's reply. Be careful to use the same register!

polite	casual
A: *Excuse me, do you have any maps?*	A: _____
B: *Yes, of course. They're right here.*	B: _____
A: _____	A: _____
B: _____	B: _____
A: _____	A: _____
B: _____	B: _____

10 Act out the phone calls (→ PB p. 88)

a) *With a partner, choose one of these situations and each one of you writes notes for one of the roles. Use the correct register.*

1. Somebody has ordered DVDs from a company, but they have not arrived yet. He / She phones the company to find out what has happened.
2. After school two teenagers have an argument about a classmate who is going out with three people who do not know about each other. – OK or not?

b) *Act out your dialogue for your class.*

11 Find the participles (→ PB p. 89; Grammar → PB G17)

a) *Underline all the adjectives in the text.*

Many <u>foreign</u> tourists go on tours of celebrity homes in Beverly Hills. They think they will see their favorite movie star at his big pool after an exciting day at the studios. But the disappointed visitors always go home without the signed photo they had hoped for. Actually, a growing number of stars now live in Malibu, where high walls and guarded gates keep the public out.

b) *Write the participles which are used as adjectives in the grid.*

present participle: _____

past participle: _____

12 Participles as adjectives (→ PB p. 90; Grammar → PB G17)

Put in the participles in the right form.

"Many people talk about their _____ (excite) vacation on a Southern Californian beach.

Well, I guess my _____ (surf) friends back home were wrong – or my _____

(ruin) week was not typical. To begin with, the beach was full – and very hot. There were too

many parents with _____ (scream) kids. One little boy shouted for hours about a

_____ (lose) toy or something. Then his mom found the _____ (miss)

toy, and I could start reading my well- _____ (earn) book. After that I heard a loud

_____ (crack) noise. Somebody had walked on my things! The _____ (follow)

day I sat in my room and tried to mend my _____ (break) sunglasses."

13 Seen in California: Finish the texts

Find the missing adjectives and write them down on the lines below.

> life-saving   heartbroken

> sun-kissed   never-ending

>> Millions of tourists *love* the (2) beaches of Santa Monica which ...

Our surf rescue teams have all the (4) equipment they need to help ...

>> It is the story of a (3) fight between aggressive businesspeople and ...

>> In this movie Susan plays the (1) girl whose boyfriend has just left her and ...

1. _____   3. _____

2. _____   4. _____

◎ 14 Listening: How to: Show strong feelings (→ PB p. 91)

a) *Look at the picture and listen to the three conversations.*
Then write down the numbers 1, 2 or 3 next to the correct conversation.

b) *Listen again. Who says what? Write down the number of the scene and the speaker (girl, boy, man).*

1. OK, OK. I only wanted to help. _____ 2. You should be more careful. _____

3. You should look where you're going! _____ 4. I guess I was in too much of a hurry. _____

15 Mediation: Alcatraz[1] – a National Park

Your neighbors are planning a trip to California. They ask you questions about this website because your English is better than theirs. They are interested in the history of the island. They also want to know how you can get to the island and what you can do and see there. Write the information they ask for in your exercise book.

TIP

Underline the information you find for the questions. Then decide which information is really important for your answers. Don't worry if you don't know all the words!

Alcatraz Island
California

Part of
Golden Gate Recreation Area

The small island of Alcatraz (15 miles off the coast of California) is so famous because of the prison which was in operation there last century. Most of the visitors (over a million every year) come to the island because they have seen Alcatraz in Hollywood action movies. But the history of Alcatraz starts long before the prison.
In 1854 the first lighthouse on the US Pacific coast was built there, in 1859 the first Army fortress on the West Coast was created there, and in 1934 the federal government took over the island and opened its new, high-tech no-escape prison for the most dangerous bad guys in the US. It was a very secret place. Prisoners were kept in their cells almost all the time, and no information was given to the public. The prison was closed in 1963, but the stories about terrible crimes and risky escapes live on. Today the island is looked after by the National Park Service for the millions of tourists – and seabirds.
The only way to get to Alcatraz is by ferry from San Francisco. There are departures about every half hour from 9:00 am, every day of the year except on Christmas Day and New Year's Day. The Alcatraz ferries often sell out quickly, especially in summer. To find out about prices and to book tickets in advance, please visit the Alcatraz Cruises website. Entrance to the island itself is free. There are numerous free videos and exhibitions, plus the cellhouse audio tour which is included in the price of the ferry ticket. The weather can be cool and foggy at any time of the year, so visitors are advised to bring warm clothing.

[1]**Alcatraz** [ˈælkətræz]

TIP
Look for keywords!

16 Revision: Tenses: The Gold Rush¹ (→ PB p. 91)

Complete the sentences with the correct tense of the verbs.
(You need a passive form for the underlined verbs.)

When gold __was discovered__ (discover) in California at the beginning of 1848, not many

white people _____ (come) to live in this Native American land yet. But

after news of the gold _____ (arrive) at the East Coast, thousands of people

there _____ (hope) that they, too, _____ (find) gold

in California. At this time the transcontinental railroad _____

(not yet build), so people _____ (must) travel by covered wagon. Today we

_____ (know) many details about these long journeys because some people,

like Amy Wilson, _____ (write) diaries while they _____

(travel) and after they _____ (arrive) in California. Between 1848 and 1850 the

population went from 20,000 to 220,000.

"Oct. 10, 1849: We have _____ (just get) to a place near Sacramento. But

_____ (we ever be able to) have a good life here?"

"Sept. 20, 1850: Papa _____

(not find) any gold for weeks now. Some people

_____ (say) that the Gold

Rush _____ (be) over. Maybe we

_____ (go) back to Chicago."

17 Revision: The passive: California's water (→ PB p. 91)

a) *The writer of the article used too many active sentences. Rewrite the underlined sentences in the passive. (You don`t always need a phrase with **by**.) Use your exercise book.*

Start like this: In the past many cars were washed every week, and grass …

In the past most people washed their cars every week, and they kept their grass green with lots of water. But now laws have been made, and special police officers, the 'water cops²', make sure people respect them. If people allow water to run from gardens into the street, they are given fines³ by the cops.

Many cities and clubs have taken away the grass from the sports fields, too. Fake grass is used now. Most people have heard that they should turn the water off when they are not using it. But will people really try to save water even when the water cops cannot see them?

b) *Compare your text with your partner's text. Have you forgotten anything?*

¹**Gold Rush** ['gəʊld rʌʃ] = Goldrausch • ²**cop** [kɒp] = *umgangssprachlich für Polizist / -in* • ³**fine** [faɪn] = Strafe

18 Drew Barrymore: What happened? (→ PB p. 94)

a) *Put these events, places, etc. in the right order. Write the numbers 1, 2, … in the boxes.*
Work in groups.

first boyfriend ___	E. T. premiere __1__	no more hanging cut with kids ___
three new schools ___	New York ___	"Out of the house, Mom!" ___
rehabilitation program ___	to hospital in a taxi ___	first visits to night clubs ___
first real summer vacation for years ___	addiction to cocaine ___	fans asking for autographs ___

b) *Which three events do you think were the most important or serious in Drew's life?*
Discuss in your group and agree on three. Compare your result with another group.

1. _____

2. _____

3. _____

19 What do you think? (→ PB p. 94)

Answer the questions. The line numbers tell you where you can find the information you need.

1. How did Drew's life suddenly change after the *E. T.* premiere? (lines 9–21)

_____

_____

2. Would you have wanted to be Drew's friend in those days? Why / why not? (lines 31–50; 63–82)

_____

_____

3. Why do you think Drew "thanked her lucky stars" for her breakdown? (lines 88–124)

_____

_____

20 Writing texts: The story of that night (→ PB p. 95)

Imagine you are the friend who came and took Drew to hospital. Tell the story of Drew's breakdown for a newspaper. Remember that the readers are interested in personal details and sensations. Use your exercise book. The Skills box on p. 38 in your Workbook can help you.

You can start like this: When I arrived at Drew's house, I could …

WRITING SKILLS

21 Setting (→ PB p. 96)

Choose one of these pictures for your story and make notes about the setting.

Where? (Region? Town? Country? Outside?)	
When? (Year? Season? Night? Before / After …?)	

22 Plot (→ PB p. 96)

a) *Make notes about the plot.*

Main idea (in one sentence)	
Characters (names, details, …)	
Highlight (mistake / rescue / success / surprise / …)	

b) *Now write the outline of your story in note form or short sentences. Leave space for more notes between the lines. Use your exercise book.*

TIP
Improve your language with conjunctions to link sentences.

23 Atmosphere (→ PB p. 96)

Add adjectives / adverbs (▲) and relative clauses (♦) to the text to make it more interesting. Use your exercise book.

In the café Ben noticed a ▲ girl ♦. He did not talk to her. She smiled at him ▲. She sat down ▲ at a ▲ table ♦. She called the waiter ♦. She wanted to order a ▲ coffee. Ben wanted to meet the girl ♦. He stood up ▲ and walked ▲ through the ▲ café. Everybody was watching.

24 Your turn: Write your own story (→ PB p. 96)

a) *Use your notes and the tip to write your own story. Don't forget the title. Use your exercise book.*

b) *Discuss your texts in groups of four. Each group chooses the best text and presents it in class.*

25 Phrasal verbs (→ PB p. 97)

Phrasal verbs are often used in casual language. Complete the text with the phrasal verbs on the right. It must have the same meaning as the verb in brackets.

check out   find out
go after   turn into
show up ✓

Hi Louise!

Dan's party was a drama! Amy __showed up__ (arrive) at six, and everybody said "Hi". Then

she _____ (examine) all the other guys apart from her own boyfriend Thomas.

Well, when Thomas noticed it, he was furious, and their argument almost _____

(become) a fight! Then Amy ran outside, and Dan _____ (follow) her. But Amy

ignored him. Later Thomas _____ (discover) that she had fallen in love with

someone else. Poor Thomas and poor Dan! See you, Becky.

26 American English and British English (→ PB p. 97)

Match the AE to the BE words.

Hey! Those are my shades [ʃeɪdz]!   **1**

I'd love to drive one of those huge trucks [trʌks]!   **2**

Your cell phone? No, sorry. Ask the janitor ['dʒænɪtər] about it.   **3**

I don't understand our History assignment [əˈsaɪnmnt].

I'll explain it to you later.   **4**

1. caretaker _____   2. homework _____

3. lorry _____   4. sunglasses _____

27 A word puzzle

1. The register for talking to friends:
2. The register for talking to your boss:
3. The opposite of 'clever':
4. Another word for a firm:
5. The opposite of 'real':
6. Where and when a story happens:
7. A visitor to your house:
8. What many people like about California:

8

1 ☐ __ __ __ __ __

2 __ __ ☐ __ __ __

3 __ __ __ __ ☐ __ __ __

4 __ __ ☐ __ __ __ __

5 __ ☐ __ __

6 __ __ __ ☐ __ __ __ __

7 __ __ ☐ __ __ __

28 Relative clauses: The Golden Gate Bridge (→ PB p. 98; Grammar → PB G16)

Turn two sentences into one.
Use relative clauses.

1. The Golden Gate Bridge is one of the sights of San Francisco.
   It was opened in 1937.

   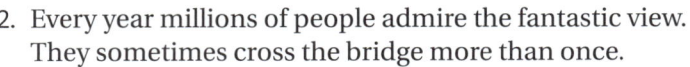
   The Golden Gate Bridge, which _____

   _____

2. Every year millions of people admire the fantastic view.
   They sometimes cross the bridge more than once.

   _____

   _____

3. But fog can be a problem for drivers. It often comes in from the ocean.

   _____

4. However, for tourists the bridge can look great even in bad weather. The tourists take photos.

   _____

   _____

29 How to: Show strong feelings (→ PB p. 98)

What can you say to someone who …

1. … keeps pushing a small boy who is waiting for the bus? – _____

2. … almost crashes into you on his / her bike? – _____

3. … takes your glass and drinks out of it? – _____

4. … keeps interrupting your conversation with a friend? – _____

30 Participles: Death Valley today (→ PB p. 98; Grammar → PB G17)

Underline the correct participle.

A (breaking • growing • losing) number of tourists is finding out that Death Valley is a(n) (interested • exciting • frightened) place to visit. (Hidden • Interesting • Experienced) campers and walkers can discover many (surprising • hiding • surprised) attractions in the desert. You must wear good walking shoes, but hot feet are better than a (saved • growing • broken) leg! If you are (interested • surprising • exciting) in history, you could visit one of the (hiding • surviving • losing) ghost towns. Tourists don't have to be (frightening • frightened • experienced) of Death Valley anymore – but they shouldn't forget those life (-opening • -saving • -hidden) water bottles!

31 The right register

Jake would like to have this job. He is talking to Mr. Lopez at the hotel, but he is using the wrong register. Rewrite his role using the polite register.

El Dorado Hotel
We are looking for a friendly teenager 13–18 to welcome[1] guests. Interested? Talk to Dave Lopez.

Dave Lopez	Jake
Good afternoon. What can I do for you?	Hi! Where's Dave? *Good afternoon. I'd like* _____
I'm Dave Lopez. How can I help you?	What about that job in your hotel here? I'm your man! _____
Could you tell me something about yourself and your qualifications?	Sure. Well, I'm a relaxed kind of guy – good with people, friendly. You know the type, I guess. _____ _____
We're looking for someone who speaks Spanish and French.	French? Oh no! But my Spanish is – *fenomenal*. _____
Could I ask you to fill in this information, please?	Sure. Give me that pen, will you? _____

32 Your US quiz   (→ PB p. 99)

a) *Write down the answers.*

1. How many boroughs are there in New York? _____

2. What color are New York cabs? _____

3. What game do the New York Yankees play? _____

4. What state is the Grand Canyon in? _____

5. Which is the highest mountain in the US? _____

6. Where did Route 66 start in the east? _____

7. What can you see from the Skywalk? _____

8. Which state has the most national parks? _____

9. What does every film star hope to win? _____

10. What hit San Francisco in 1906? _____

11. What is the AE word for 'rubbish'? _____

12. What is the AE word for 'queue'? _____

b) *Write down the last letter of each answer.* _____
Then use the letters to fill in the spaces below.

You have found out a lot about this during the school year:

T ☐ ☐   ☐ M ☐ ☐ I C ☐ ☐   ☐ A ☐   ☐ F   ☐ I F ☐

[1] **to welcome** [ˈwelkəm] = empfangen

〈Revision〉 Unit 3–5

1 Opposites

alive   dry   stupid   wonderful   illegal   reckless   heartless   private

a) *Write the words in the boxes next to their opposites.*

1. careful _____ 2. kind _____ 3. wet _____ 4. legal _____

5. public _____ 6. clever _____ 7. terrible _____ 8. dead _____

b) *Make a sentence with each pair. Use your exercise book.*

2 The infinitive after superlatives

There was a party at Mel's house yesterday. Today Emma is still not happy,
Ben is very tired and Dustin is still very excited. Write a sentence for each picture
and write down the reason for Emma's, Ben's and Dustin's feelings.

Use the first • the last • the only one ... *and the infinitive.*

Emma **1**   Ben **2**   Dustin **3**   Ben **4**

1. _Emma was the only one_ _____

2. _____

3. _____

4. _____

3 What can you say in these situations?

1. You see someone crossing the road without looking. _____

2. Your sister has taken your cell phone. _____

3. Somebody is kicking the back of your seat. _____

4. Four boys are bullying a small boy. _____

4   Make your language more interesting

Turn one of the sentences into a non-defining relative clause.

1. The beaches of Malibu are some of California's most beautiful places to swim, have a picnic or go surfing. They are also very well-known from many Hollywood movies.

    _____

    _____

2. But some of these beaches have been closed to the public for over 20 years and will finally reopen for next week. Rich homeowners had wrongly thought of them as their own 'private' beaches.

    _____

    _____

    _____

3. Many Malibu homeowners are of course not happy about this. Their beach homes are some of the most expensive in the state.

    _____

    _____

4. But John Scott and other surfers from the Southern California Surfing Club are all very pleased about the news. They had been fighting to reopen the beaches.

    _____

    _____

5   A visitor!

A visitor arrives at your house. What can you say? Fill in the grid below with casual and polite phrases.

casual	polite
Hi! Come in.	_____ _____
Do you want a drink?	_____
_____ _____	There was some interesting news about the Malibu beaches today, wasn't there?
_____	Excuse me, could you repeat that, please?

Congratulations! Now you've worked through your whole book. Fill in your *Portfolio* again – what went well, and what could still be improved?

〈La Línea[1]〉

In this novel, two Mexican teenagers are trying to get to the US to be with their parents again who had left Mexico before them.

Of course Javi had a plan for getting on the train. He asked us to run through the steps ten times before he was satisfied[2]. I didn't understand why we had to practice jumping onto the *mata gente*[3].
5 We were young and quick and there was no one else who would try to fight us for a place on a car ladder[4].

"It's coming!" Javi said. "Can you hear it?" At that moment, we could hear the *mata gente's*
10 whistle. It was close, very close.

"Let's go!" Javi shouted. Elena was in front.

Suddenly, the *mata gente* came towards us, a giant train with whirling[5] steel wheels. It was moving much faster than I'd imagined, and we
15 would have just one chance.

"Elena! Elena! Faster. *¡Más rápido*[6]*!* I shouted.

I looked back over my shoulder. Javier was behind me.

Elena ran even faster and jumped onto the
20 lowest rung[7] of a car ladder. She hung on with one hand, and shouted, "Miguel, come on!"

She held out her free hand.

"Go, Miguel," Javier spoke into my ear. "Now!"

I grabbed the rung with one hand, Elena's
25 hand with the other. We moved up the ladder and Javi followed us.

The train went around the corner and then, from the grass, a crowd of people began to throw themselves at the *mata gente*. They ran and
30 pushed.

Some managed to get on, others didn't. A young man and woman, Javi's friends, tried, too. The husband told his wife to go faster. But she never had a chance, so they didn't make it.
35 It was over as fast as it began. The train drove on. Javi, Elena, and I crawled[8] to the top of the car and lay down, Elena lay between Javi and me. We all held hands.

It got dark and we could see the moon. The
40 *mata gente* moved us along. Javi took a rope from his bag, tied us together through our belts[9] and attached the rope to a car. Javi made us as safe as he could.

The other *mata gente* hoppers[10], most of them young children, sat on the cars in front of us, like
45 little birds on a tree out in a storm. We weren't able to talk because it was too hard to hear.

"No train gangs so far," Javi spoke into my ear. "Rest some[11]! I'll watch out for a while."

I lay down and watched the moon. I tried to
50 sleep, but I couldn't. Javi thought we could make it at least halfway to the border on the *mata gente*.

I woke up for the third time when the train's brakes screeched[12]. I was thrown to the front of the car. The train slowed down. Javi took off
55 the rope. He climbed down the ladder on the side of the car and looked out to see what was happening.

"I can't see what's happening up there," Javi said. "Can you see anything from the top?"
60 We stood up. People ran along the tops of the cars toward us. Others went down the side ladders as fast as they could.

People were shouting, "*¡La migra*[13]*!* Get off! Run!"
65 We climbed quickly down our ladder and jumped off the train. We ran into a forest[14] and watched. The *migra* caught the slowest ones, but didn't try to find the rest. When the train drove on, they had left, and we were back in our place
70 on top.

For the next two days, the *mata gente* was home. Five more times we jumped off because we didn't want to get caught by *la migra*.

But by the evening of the second day, we'd
75 only had a little bit of water from one bottle and two small *bolillos*[15] to share. We were hungry and dead tired.

We had to duck[16] again and again. There were lots of electrical wires[17]. If we touched[18] one, we'd
80 die, just like that. And the diesel smoke made it hard for us to breathe[19].

"I can't go on," Elena was tired. She shouted

---

[1] **la línea** = *Span.* line, border • [2] **satisfied** ['sætɪsfaɪd] = *here:* think that it's been enough • [3] **mata gente** = *Span. here:* name of a train (that kills people) • [4] **car ladder** [kɑː 'lædə] = Leiter an einem Waggon • [5] **whirling** ['wɜːlɪŋ] = moving and turning very fast • [6] **¡Más rápido!** = *Span.* faster • [7] **rung** [rʌŋ] = Leitersprosse • [8] **to crawl** [krɔːl] = to move on all fours • [9] **belt** [belt] = Gürtel • [10] **hopper** ['hɒpə] = sb who jumps • [11] **Rest some!** ['rest sm] = Sleep a bit! • [12] **to screech** [skriːtʃ] = to make a very high and loud sound • [13] **la migra** = *Span.* border police • [14] **forest** ['fɒrɪst] = area with lots of trees • [15] **bolillo** = *Span.* small bread • [16] **to duck** [dʌk] = almost like sitting, but you are still on your feet • [17] **wire** [waɪə] = Kabel • [18] **to touch** [tʌtʃ] = *here:* to get too close • [19] **to breathe** [briːð] = to let air in and out of your nose / mouth

above the roar[20] of the engine. "I need to eat
85 something. I need to drink. I want a bed!"
"Don't worry," Javi called back. "I've heard that
there'll be some people who will take care of
migrants like us when we arrive. We'll get some
food."
90 Elena didn't believe him. "Fairy tales[21] are for
little girls," she screamed above the roar of the
engine. "I hate this stupid train!"
The train slowed again. If we had to hop
off and on here, just one more time, one of us
95 wouldn't make it. I hadn't seen Javi rest at all.
He'd been looking out for every big and little
danger day and night. I couldn't understand how
he could still be awake[22].
The *mata gente* slowed even more, but did not
100 stop.
Elena shook her head again. "I'm getting off
here and I'm not getting back on."
And then I saw people standing at the side
of the tracks. They were throwing things at
105 the train, rocks, I thought. Maybe they hated
migrants like us in this *pueblito*[23]. We lay down
on top of the car. But nothing fell on us.

Then, I heard a girl laughing.
I looked around. There, next to the train, was
a fit man, around forty I thought. "Here!" he
shouted. "Catch[24]!"
More people came running from their houses,
their arms full. They threw things. I caught a bag
of *tortillas*. An old woman held up a water bottle,
a young girl a bag with fruit. Javi grabbed both.
Elena caught some bread. Everyone on
the top of the train got something: bread,
sandwiches, drinks and even clothes.
All up and down the train, the migrants
shouted, "¡*Gracias*[25]! ¡*Gracias*!"

So there we were, Elena and I, making that trip.
¿*Y para qué*[26]? How many times had we already
escaped death[27]? And we hadn't even arrived at
the border.
Well, I'd only been half alive anyway, for a
long time. Papá took a big part of me with him
to California when he left. He thought he was
sending for me now, but I'd already been there
and he didn't even know it.

110

115

120

125

adapted from *La línea* by Ann Jaramillo

---

[20]**roar** [rɔ:] = dark, loud noise • [21]**fairy tale** ['feəri teil] = story with witches and kings etc. • [22]**awake** [ə'weik] = not sleeping •
[23]**pueblito** = *Span.* small village • [24]**Catch!** [kætʃ] = Get it! • [25]**gracias** = *Span.* Thank you. • [26]¿**Y para qué**? = *Span.* And what
is it for? • [27]**escaped death** [ɪ,skeipt 'deθ] = *here:* managed not to die

---

1 Before you read

a) *What do you already know about the border between Mexico and the US?*
How do illegal immigrants try to get across borders?

b) *Look at these lines from the text:* "For the next two days, the *mata gente* (the people killer) was
home." *What do you expect will happen in the story? Work with a partner.*

2 Working with the text

a) "Javi already had a plan for getting us on the train."
*Imagine you are Javi and you tell Elena and Miguel exactly what they have to do. Underline the
different steps in the text. Write what Javi says in your exercise book.*

b) *Make notes about the characters in the list. Which character do you like best? Say why.*

Javi: _____

Miguel: _____

Elena: _____

c) *They have to sit on the train for two days and just wait to get closer to the border. Write one extra
page of text in your exercise book in which you say how they spend their time. Use the I-narrator[28]
from the story.*

---

[28]**narrator** [nə'reitə] = the person who tells the story to the reader

GROUP SKILLS

You already know different kinds of group work: role plays, discussions, presentations. Team activities are also a good way to find out about a topic because the work can be shared in the group.

1 Organize your group work

a) *Work in a group of five on this topic:*

Activities for young people in the five boroughs of New York City.

Decide who is going to deal with which area and fill in the grid.

name	borough

b) *Then make a KFL grid: Write down what your group already knows about the five boroughs and what you want to find out. Use your exercise book.*

2 Find out about one part of the topic

Each one in the group now joins a new group of students who want to deal with the same borough.
Collect all the information you already have about your borough. Discuss what information is still missing. Decide where you can get it (Internet, library …) and who is going to do it. When you have all finished your research in this group, make an ad for your borough on a poster.

3 A gallery walk

a) *Put the posters on the classroom wall. Go back to your first group. Then each group does its own gallery walk and talks about the posters.*

b) *In the grid write down three important things you learned about each borough and decide which borough is your favorite one.*

The Bronx	Queens	Manhattan	Staten Island	Brooklyn

WRITING SKILLS

Everybody should check their notes and texts carefully, but it is a good idea to ask a partner to check, too. He / She can sometimes see more easily what is missing, or what is wrong because he / she does not know the text. This skill can help you and your partner to correct your texts and to improve them.

TIP

Watch out for …
- 3rd person sg 's'
- adjectives / adverbs
- irregular verbs
- word order
- …

1 Comparing ideas

In your class you are all preparing texts about your favorite school sport.

a) *Read what someone else wrote. Is there anything missing? Add your suggestions on the right.*

Basketball

rules ☐

very popular ☐

history ☐

basketball at our school ☐

why you like it ☐

why it is so popular ☐

b) *Suggest a good order for the text. Write numbers next to the notes (with your suggestions).*

c) *Now make your own notes about a sport and show them to a partner and ask for his / her suggestions. Use your exercise book.*

2 Correct someone else's text

a) *Read this text which someone else has written. Underline the parts of the text which you want to comment on and then make notes on the right. Then compare them with your partner's notes.*

l. 1: more information (When / …?)

The beginnings of basketball

Basketball was invented by <u>James Naismith</u>. They wanted an inside team game for winter.
At first a soccer ball was used. Teams had nine players. (Today they have five.) Four years later
5 the game had become popular at US colleges. During the 20th century it became popular all over the world. Basketball became a professional sport in about 1900, and the NBA was formed in 1949.

b) *What can you say to the person who wrote the text? Use your notes and the Useful phrases.*

TIP

When you make comments on a text, you want to be helpful and improve it.
- Say what you think, but remember to be polite and friendly.
- Say something nice about the text, too.

USEFUL PHRASES

I like the story, but …
The facts are interesting …
Have you checked …?
I would use more …
… is missing.

I don't understand …
I'd like to know more about …
What do you mean by …?
It would be even better if …
I think you should use …

1 Pronunciation of words

It is important to know where the stress of a word is.

a) *Read these words out loud and put a (') before the part which is stressed.*

amazing • delicious • elevator • engineer • expectation • immigrant • interrupt • principal • terrorist

b) *Listen to the CD and check. Correct any words you got wrong.*

TIP
Remember: It's important to listen carefully to learn to speak good English.

Into'nation

2 Phrases and sentences

Groups of words and whole sentences also have stressed and unstressed parts.

a) **Link the words:** *Underline the words that begin with vowels[1].*
Listen to the CD and check the way the words are linked. Then read the sentence out loud and link the words in the same way.

Who do you think I met in the park at three in the afternoon?

b) **Sentence stress:** *Listen to the following sentence:*

Karen didn't say Tracy stole the money from her dad.

The sentence is read six times on the CD and the main stress is put on different words. How does this change the meaning? Complete this chart.

main stress	meaning	main stress	meaning
1. Karen	Another person said it.	4. stole	
2. say		5. money	
3. Tracy		6. dad	

c) **Intonation[2]:** *A different intonation can give a sentence a different meaning.*

1. *Work with a partner. Take turns saying the following sentence in two different ways. Your partner will check your intonation.*

Linda is the new volleyball trainer.

Intonation 1: You have just heard that Linda Webb, a brilliant and popular player, is your new trainer.
Intonation 2: Imagine that your partner has told you that Linda, the biggest idiot in the sports club, is the new trainer.

2. *Then listen to the CD and check.*

3. *Take turns with a partner. Read each of these sentences with two different kinds of intonation. Your partner must explain what you mean or how you feel.*

It looks like a really expensive T-shirt.   I don't often agree with Laura about music.

You don't know who I am.   Tracy doesn't want to see the movie again.

[1] **vowel** [vaʊəl] = Vokal • [2] **intonation** [ˌɪntəˈneɪʃn] = Intonation, Satzbetonung

VOCABULARY SKILLS

You know how to use an English-German dictionary. Now find out how an English-English dictionary (English words explained in English) can help you. (→ PB p. 164)

1 Understanding an English-English dictionary

Look at this dictionary text. Try to explain the letters and words.

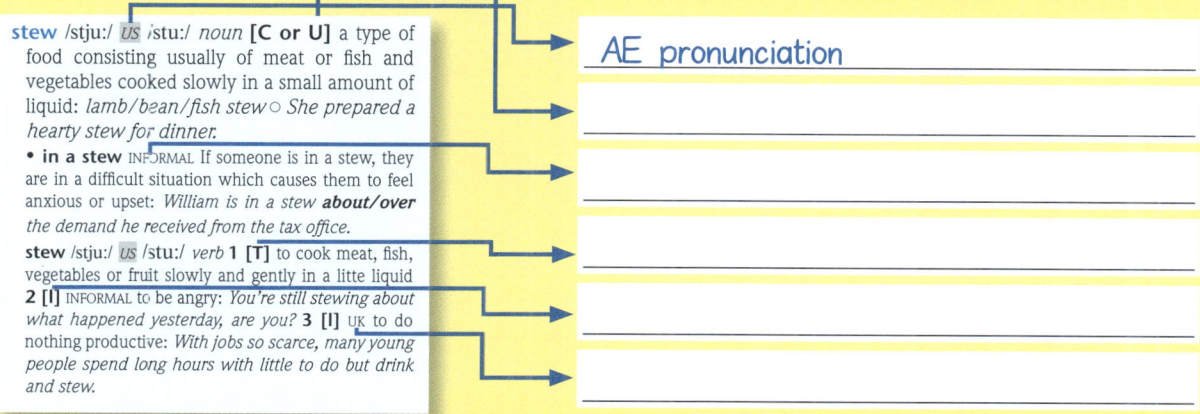

stew /stju:/ *US* /stu:/ *noun* **[C or U]** a type of food consisting usually of meat or fish and vegetables cooked slowly in a small amount of liquid: *lamb/bean/fish stew* ○ *She prepared a hearty stew for dinner.*
• **in a stew** INFORMAL If someone is in a stew, they are in a difficult situation which causes them to feel anxious or upset: *William is in a stew about/over the demand he received from the tax office.*
stew /stju:/ *US* /stu:/ *verb* **1** **[T]** to cook meat, fish, vegetables or fruit slowly and gently in a litte liquid **2** **[I]** INFORMAL to be angry: *You're still stewing about what happened yesterday, are you?* **3** **[I]** UK to do nothing productive: *With jobs so scarce, many young people spend long hours with little to do but drink and stew.*

AE pronunciation

2 How an English-English dictionary can help you

a) **Reading**

Read this sentence.

Nobody will be admitted after the movie has started.

Of course, 'admit' does not mean 'zugeben' here. Underline the correct meaning of 'admit' for this sentence in the dictionary text. Then write down how you would say the sentence in German.

admit ALLOW IN /əd'mɪt/ *verb* **[T]** (-tt-) **1** to allow someone to enter a place: *Each ticket admits one member and one guest.* ○ *Men will not be admitted to the restaurant without a tie.* ○ LITERARY *A gap between the curtains admitted the faint glimmer of a street lamp.* **2** to allow a person or country to join an organization: *Spain was admitted to the European Community in 1936.* **3** to allow someone to enter a hospital because they need medical care: *She was admitted to hospital (US to the hospital) suffering from shock.*

b) **Writing**

1. *Ritchie says, 'I'd like to hit the slopes'. Can you say 'Let's hit the swimming pool / the café'? Check the dictionary text on the right.*

2. *You want to write a text about an unusual rock festival. You have made these notes:*

6:00 • Shauna • go home • brother • huge music festival • house / garden • parents arrive • very angry • next day • 100 phone calls • reporters • 'your brother's big story!'

Write the text and try to use two more phrases with 'hit'. Use your exercise book.

Start like this: At 6:00 Shauna decided to hit …

hit REACH /hɪt/ *verb* **[T]** (hitting, hit, hit) **1** to arrive at a place or position: *If we turn left at the next junction, we should hit the main road after five miles or so.* **2** to succeed in reaching or achieving something: *Our profits hit an all-time high of £20 million last year.* ○ *I just can't hit (= sing) those high notes like I used to.*
• **hit the bottle** to start to drink too much alcohol
• **hit the ceiling/roof** to become extremely angry: *Dad'll hit the ceiling when he finds out I've left school.*
• **hit the deck** to lie down quickly and suddenly so that you are hidden from view or sheltered from something dangerous
• **hit the ground running** to immediately work hard and successfully at a new activity
• **hit the hay/sack** INFORMAL to go to bed in order to sleep: *I've got a busy day tomorrow, so I think I'll hit the sack.*
• **hit the headlines** to appear in the news suddenly or receive a lot of attention in news reports: *He hit the headlines two years ago when he was arrested for selling drugs to the Prime Minister's nephew.*
• **hit the road** to leave a place or begin a journey: *I'd love to stay longer but I must be hitting the road.*
• **hit the spot** to be exactly what is needed: *That bacon sandwich really hit the spot!*

READING SKILLS

You already know some reading skills. Skimming and scanning are used to get the main ideas and information quickly. Then you can use other skills to find out more details.

1 Skimming and scanning

Why don't you let Norton Travel organize your unforgettable vacation in the far North of America? Our most popular <mark>annual</mark> trip is in July. It offers families a <mark>unique</mark> chance to experience a mountain region of the US which has an amazing number of different animals, although it's under snow and in darkness for much of the year. But in summer it never gets really dark, so you have lots of time for sightseeing.

On the first day you arrive at your hotel in Anchorage[1]. Spend the afternoon checking out the zoo or one of the town's museums, or have a swim in the hotel pool. Those of you who are interested in other kinds of <mark>aquatic</mark> activities can look forward to our first journey – to the town of Whittier[2], where there is boating and rafting for every taste.

The big highlight is the boat trip to see more than twenty <mark>glaciers</mark>. Remember, this is one of the few

places in the world where it's still possible to experience glaciers.

On our next trip we drive towards a small town. You'll always want to keep your camera ready because in clear weather Mount McKinley (North America's highest mountain) is <mark>visible</mark> from the road! For the last part of our trip we go on a guided motor coach tour around a particularly interesting part of Denali[3] National Park. After one night at a mountain lodge, we go back to Anchorage for the last day. Every year we <mark>receive</mark> letters and e-mails from people telling us how much they enjoyed their trip with us. Experience the far North of America with us! Norton Travel!

[1] **Anchorage** ['æŋkrɪdʒ] • [2] **Whittier** ['wɪtɪə] • [3] **Denali** [də'nɑ:li]

a) *Read this text from a website quickly, then say what it is about in one sentence. (Skimming)*

b) *Look at the text again. Tick the topics which are dealt with in the text. (Scanning)*

money/costs ☐   transport ☐   offer – more information ☐

disadvantages ☐   food ☐   places to stay ☐

TIP

You don't need to understand everything. Concentrate on the words and phrases you know.

2 Words from other languages

Guess the meaning of the yellow words. Are they like French, Spanish or Latin words you know?

	languages and words	German
annual ['ænju:əl]	Fr.: année, annuel;	jährlich
unique [ju:'ni:k]		
aquatic [ə'kwætɪk]		
glaciers ['glæsɪəz]		
visible ['vɪzɪbl]		
receive [rɪ'si:v]		

〈A game〉 US road trip

YOU NEED

and a

You and your friends are on a coast-to-coast trip through the US. There are 2–4 players and one referee who reads out the questions and checks the answers on page 86. The youngest player starts. Answer the questions or follow the instructions. If your answer is correct, you can stay where you are. If your answer is wrong, you must go back three spaces. The player who arrives at FINISH first wins.

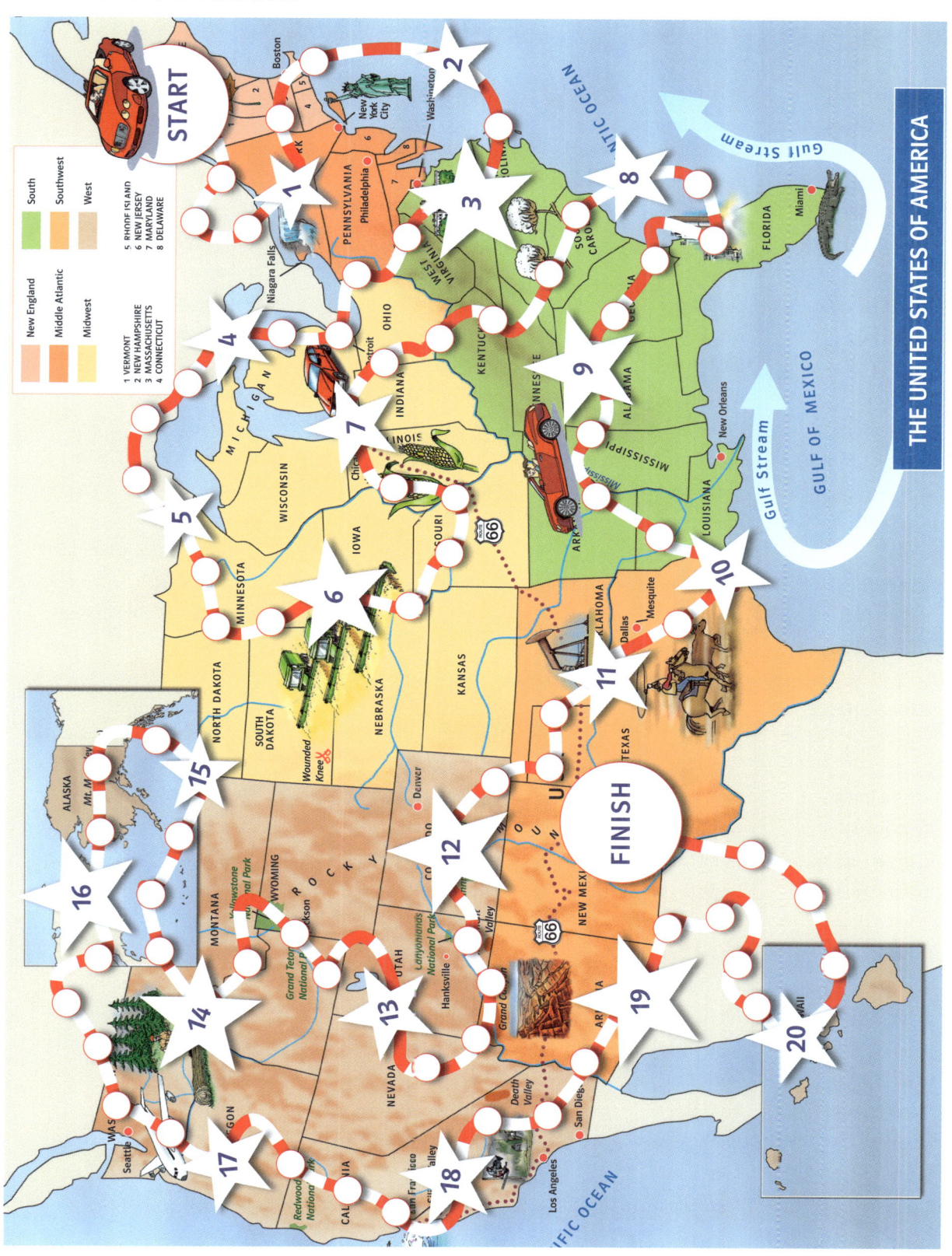

List of irregular verbs

infinitive	simple past	past participle	German
to **be** [biː]	**was/were** [wɒz, wɜː]	**been** [biːn]	sein
to **become** [bɪˈkʌm]	**became** [bɪˈkeɪm]	**become** [bɪˈkʌm]	werden
to **begin** [bɪˈgɪn]	**began** [bɪˈgæn]	**begun** [bɪˈgʌn]	beginnen
to **bleed** [bliːd]	**bled** [bled]	**bled** [bled]	bluten
to **break** [breɪk]	**broke** [brəʊk]	**broken** [ˈbrəʊkn]	(zer)brechen; kaputtmachen
to **bring** [brɪŋ]	**brought** [brɔːt]	**brought** [brɔːt]	(mit)bringen
to **build** [bɪld]	**built** [bɪlt]	**built** [bɪlt]	bauen
to **burn** [bɜːn]	**burnt/burned** [bɜːnt, bɜːnd]	**burnt/burned** [bɜːnt, bɜːnd]	(ver)brennen
to **buy** [baɪ]	**bought** [bɔːt]	**bought** [bɔːt]	kaufen
to **catch** [kætʃ]	**caught** [kɔːt]	**caught** [kɔːt]	fangen
to **choose** [tʃuːz]	**chose** [tʃəʊz]	**chosen** [ˈtʃəʊzn]	(aus)wählen
to **come** [kʌm]	**came** [keɪm]	**come** [kʌm]	kommen
to **cost** [kɒst]	**cost** [kɒst]	**cost** [kɒst]	kosten
to **cut** [kʌt]	**cut** [kʌt]	**cut** [kʌt]	(sich) schneiden
to **deal** (with) [diːl]	**dealt** [dealt]	**dealt** [dealt]	(be)handeln
to **do** [duː]	**did** [dɪd]	**done** [dʌn]	machen, tun
to **draw** [drɔː]	**drew** [druː]	**drawn** [drɔːn]	zeichnen
to **drink** [drɪŋk]	**drank** [dræŋk]	**drunk** [drʌŋk]	trinken
to **drive** [draɪv]	**drove** [drəʊv]	**driven** [ˈdrɪvn]	fahren
to **eat** [iːt]	**ate** [et, eɪt]	**eaten** [ˈiːtn]	essen
to **fall** [fɔːl]	**fell** [fel]	**fallen** [ˈfɔːlən]	(herunter)fallen, hinfallen
to **feel** [fiːl]	**felt** [felt]	**felt** [felt]	(sich) fühlen
to **fight** [faɪt]	**fought** [fɔːt]	**fought** [fɔːt]	kämpfen, (sich) streiten
to **find** [faɪnd]	**found** [faʊnd]	**found** [faʊnd]	finden
to **fly** [flaɪ]	**flew** [fluː]	**flown** [fləʊn]	fliegen
to **forget** [fəˈget]	**forgot** [fəˈgɒt]	**forgotten** [fəˈgɒtn]	vergessen
to **get** [get]	**got** [gɒt]	**got** [gɒt]	holen, bringen; (be)kommen; werden
to **give** [gɪv]	**gave** [geɪv]	**given** [ˈgɪvn]	geben
to **go** [gəʊ]	**went** [went]	**gone** [gɒn]	gehen
to **grow** [grəʊ]	**grew** [gruː]	**grown** [grəʊn]	wachsen
to **hang** [hæŋ]	**hung** [hʌŋ]	**hung** [hʌŋ]	hängen
to **have** [hæv]	**had** [hæd]	**had** [hæd]	haben
to **hear** [hɪə]	**heard** [hɜːd]	**heard** [hɜːd]	hören
to **hide** [haɪd]	**hid** [hɪd]	**hidden** [ˈhɪdn]	(sich) verstecken
to **hit** [hɪt]	**hit** [hɪt]	**hit** [hɪt]	schlagen; treffen
to **hold** [həʊld]	**held** [held]	**held** [held]	halten
to **hurt** [hɜːt]	**hurt** [hɜːt]	**hurt** [hɜːt]	verletzen, weh tun
to **keep** [kiːp]	**kept** [kept]	**kept** [kept]	behalten
to **know** [nəʊ]	**knew** [njuː]	**known** [nəʊn]	wissen; kennen
to **lay** [leɪ]	**laid** [leɪd]	**laid** [leɪd]	legen
to **learn** [lɜːn]	**learnt/learned** [lɜːnt, lɜːnd]	**learnt/learned** [lɜːnt, lɜːnd]	lernen

infinitive	simple past	past participle	German
to **lend** [lend]	**lent** [lent]	**lent** [lent]	leihen
to **let** [let]	**let** [let]	**let** [let]	lassen
to **lie** [laɪ]	**lay** [leɪ]	**lain** [leɪn]	liegen
to **lose** [lu:z]	**lost** [lɒst]	**lost** [lɒst]	verlieren
to **make** [meɪk]	**made** [meɪd]	**made** [meɪd]	machen, tun
to **mean** [mi:n]	**meant** [ment]	**meant** [ment]	bedeuten; meinen
to **meet** [mi:t]	**met** [met]	**met** [met]	(sich) treffen
to **pay** [peɪ]	**paid** [peɪd]	**paid** [peɪd]	(be)zahlen
to **put** [pʊt]	**put** [pʊt]	**put** [pʊt]	setzen, stellen, legen
to **read** [ri:d]	**read** [red]	**read** [red]	lesen
to **ride** [raɪd]	**rode** [rəʊd]	**ridden** ['rɪdn]	fahren, reiten
to **ring** [rɪŋ]	**rang** [ræŋ]	**rung** [rʌŋ]	klingeln, läuten
to **run** [rʌn]	**ran** [ræn]	**run** [rʌn]	rennen, laufen
to **say** [seɪ]	**said** [sed]	**said** [sed]	sagen
to **see** [si:]	**saw** [sɒ:]	**seen** [si:n]	sehen
to **sell** [sel]	**sold** [səʊld]	**sold** [səʊld]	verkaufen
to **send** [send]	**sent** [sent]	**sent** [sent]	schicken
to **shake** [ʃeɪk]	**shook** [ʃʊk]	**shaken** ['ʃeɪkn]	schütteln
to **shine** [ʃaɪn]	**shone** [ʃɒn]	**shone** [ʃɒn]	scheinen; glänzen
to **shoot** [ʃu:t]	**shot** [ʃɒt]	**shot** [ʃɒt]	schießen
to **show** [ʃəʊ]	**showed** [ʃəʊd]	**shown** [ʃəʊn]	zeigen
to **sing** [sɪŋ]	**sang** [sæŋ]	**sung** [sʌŋ]	singen
to **sink** [sɪŋk]	**sank** [sæŋk]	**sunk** [sʌŋk]	sinken
to **sit** [sɪt]	**sat** [sæt]	**sat** [sæt]	sitzen
to **sleep** [sli:p]	**slept** [slept]	**slept** [slept]	schlafen
to **smell** [smel]	**smelt/smelled** [smelt, smeld]	**smelt/smelled** [smelt, smeld]	riechen
to **speak** [spi:k]	**spoke** [spəʊk]	**spoken** ['spəʊkn]	sprechen
to **spend** [spend]	**spent** [spent]	**spent** [spent]	ausgeben, verbringen
to **stand** [stænd]	**stood** [stʊd]	**stood** [stʊd]	stehen
to **steal** [sti:l]	**stole** [stəʊl]	**stolen** ['stəʊlən]	stehlen
to **swim** [swɪm]	**swam** [swæm]	**swum** [swʌm]	schwimmen
to **take** [teɪk]	**took** [tʊk]	**taken** ['teɪkn]	(mit)nehmen, bringen
to **teach** [ti:tʃ]	**taught** [tɔ:t]	**taught** [tɔ:t]	lehren
to **tell** [tel]	**told** [təʊld]	**told** [təʊld]	erzählen, sagen
to **think** [θɪŋk]	**thought** [θɔ:t]	**thought** [θɔ:t]	denken, glauben
to **throw** [θrəʊ]	**threw** [θru:]	**thrown** [θrəʊn]	werfen
to **understand** [ˌʌndə'stænd]	**understood** [ˌʌndə'stʊd]	**understood** [ˌʌndə'stʊd]	verstehen
to **wake** [weɪk]	**woke** [wəʊk]	**woken** ['wəʊkn]	(auf)wecken; (auf)wachen
to **wear** [weə]	**wore** [wɔ:]	**worn** [wɔ:n]	anhaben, tragen
to **win** [wɪn]	**won** [wʌn]	**won** [wʌn]	gewinnen, siegen
to **write** [raɪt]	**wrote** [rəʊt]	**written** ['rɪtn]	schreiben

Lösungen Check-out

Unit 1 Seite 14

Check-out 1

31 Do a quiz about New York (→ PB p. 26)

Answer the questions without your book. All the information is somewhere in Unit 1 or on the map at the back of your book.

1. How many boroughs are there in New York City? – *There are five boroughs.*
2. How many people live in New York City? – *Eight million people live there.*
3. What is special about the cabs in New York? – *They are yellow.*
4. What kind of sports do the New York Yankees play? – *They play baseball.*
5. Where is the immigration center? – *It is on Ellis Island.*
6. In what year did terrorists attack the World Trade Center? – *They attacked it in 2001.*

32 Make sentences with the present perfect progressive (→ PB p. 26; Grammar → PB G1, 2)

Find the correct ideas and complete what Diego and his family say.

[shout at each other 6:00 • cook over twenty minutes • talk on the phone ages • sit near the door • you got up]

1. Diego: Elena! Other people want to call their friends, too, you know. *You've been talking on the phone for ages.*
2. Elena: It's your job to take the dog out this morning, Rob. Look, he's waiting. *He's been sitting near the door since you got up.*
3. Rob: I wish the people in the apartment above us would be quiet. *They've been shouting at each other since 6:00.*
4. Wife: Hey, Diego! Who's the cook here? You forgot about the eggs! *They've been cooking for over twenty minutes.*

33 Describe the situation (→ PB p. 26; Grammar → PB G3)

Suddenly yesterday evening there was no power in the Moises' apartment. Write down what they had been doing before they had to stop. Look at what they say to find out. Find your own verbs.

1. Maudeline: I was only on page 6! *She had been reading a book.*
2. Wilfred: No power – no computer game! *He had been playing a computer game.*
3. Grandma: My favorite soap had just started. *She had been watching TV.*
4. Cathia: I couldn't finish my project. *She had been doing a project.*
5. Grandad: Only half of the quiz is done! *He had been doing a quiz.*

Unit 1 Seite 15

Check-out 1

34 What are they saying or thinking? (→ PB p. 27) (Lösungsvorschlag)

Look at the pictures and put the people's feelings into words.

1. *This is the best moment of my life. I feel like I'm on top of the world.*
2. *It's very sad to see animals with no home. I wish I could take him home with me.*
3. *Wow! That's amazing. I've never felt so good and free!*
4. *I'd never have thought it! I didn't expect to find it again.*

35 Put the sentence parts in the right order (→ PB p. 27; Grammar → PB G5,6)

1. The New York subway … very • in the morning • is • busy • usually
   The New York subway is usually very busy in the morning.
2. Many thousands … make • full • of passengers • extremely • the trains
   Many thousands of passengers make the trains extremely full.
3. Often … enough • for everyone • there • seats • are not
   Often there are not enough seats for everyone.
4. A few people … to get to a seat • push • first • in front of others • always
   A few people always push in front of others to get to a seat first.
5. Other passengers … selfish • find • the way • pretty • they behave
   Other passengers find the way they behave pretty selfish.

36 Use the correct word in the correct form: adjective or adverb (→ PB p. 27)

angry • quick • good • rude • patient • hard

Breakfast in Diego's Diner always tastes *good*. Diego also works *hard* to try and give you your food *quickly*. But he can't serve everyone right away, so sometimes you have to be *patient*. It isn't a good idea to make Diego *angry*. When a customer shouted *rudely* at him yesterday, he threw the customer out!

Unit 2 Seite 27

2 Check-out

16 Use modal verbs and the perfect infinitive (→ PB p. 42, Grammar → PB G7) *(Lösungsv.)*

Kelly is waiting for her boyfriend outside a café.
What does she think in these situations?

1. Her boyfriend Zack has not arrived for their date.
   (can't • forget) "_He can't have forgotten our date!_"

2. It is getting cold outside.
   (should • wear) "_I should have worn warmer clothes._"

3. Her cell phone is not in her bag.
   (must • leave) "_I must have left it somewhere._"

4. Zack arrives with flowers and says, "Sorry, I'm late."
   (should • be patient) "_I should have been more patient._"

17 The passive infinitive (→ PB p. 42, Grammar → PB G10)

Cody: "I hope they'll choose me for the team." ①

Tiffany: "I hope somebody will invite me to the dance." ②

Brittany: "Maybe Mom and Dad will take me out for dinner." ③

Jose: "I guess they'll pay me well for my work here." ④

Use want • would like • expect • hope with the passive infinitive.

1. Cody _hopes to be chosen for the team._
2. Tiffany _hopes to be invited to the dance._
3. Brittany _would like to be taken out for dinner._
4. _Jose expects to be paid well for his work._

18 Use modals and the passive infinitive (→ PB p. 42, Grammar → PB G9) *(Lösungsvorschlag)*

What information do these pictures give?

① ② ③ ④ Cafe

1. _Cars may / can be parked here._
2. _Cell phones must not be used here._
3. _Helmets must be worn here._
4. _Coffee can be bought here._

twenty-seven **27**

Unit 3 Seite 40

3 Check-out

23 Put in the gerunds (→ PB p. 60, Grammar → PB G9)

| fish | see | go | listen | ski | visit | ride | relax |

The winters in Jackson are great, but have you seen our summers? If you like _skiing_ in the mountains, you will love _going_ on hikes in them in the summer, too. Or maybe _riding_ a horse is more your thing! Or if you just enjoy _relaxing_ in the fresh mountain air, _listening_ to a concert at our music festival in July is a great idea. _Fishing_ in our mountain rivers is another popular activity. Many tourists spend their whole vacation _visiting_ the national parks near Jackson. We look forward to _seeing_ you in Jackson – at any time of the year!

24 Choose the correct prepositions

I had always dreamed _of_ meeting Mr. Right. But I was not very good _at_ meeting new people. And I was tired _of_ going on dates with friends of friends. Then one day I was at the supermarket and I was just talking to the cashier _about_ the weather. He told me he loved skiing and did not feel _like_ spending another winter without snow and mountains. I told him I was interested _in_ skiing, too, and thinking _of_ moving to a new place with mountains. It was so easy to talk to him and I live in Jackson, Wyoming, with lots of snow and mountains. So my advice is: keep _on_ dreaming and do not give _up_ hoping! You can look forward _to_ meeting your Mr. or Mrs. Right, too!

25 Complete the sentences with object + ing-forms (→ PB p. 60, Grammar → PB G10)

1. Dean is out in the car. Now it's snowing. I'm worried about …
   him having an accident.

2. Dustin has invited his friends to his house. He is looking forward to …
   them coming.

3. Richie's parents always tell him to get good grades. He hates …
   them telling him to get good grades.

4. Sylvia gets e-mails from her friends every night. She loves …
   them sending her e-mails.

40 *forty*

Unit 4 Seite 53

Check-out 4

19 Complete the sentences with an object and infinitive (→ PB p. 76; Grammar → PB G14)

Please stop!

Smile, everyone!

Go away!

Warmer water would be nicer!
Brrr!

Take it with you!

1. The hiker wants _the rain to stop._
2. The boy would like _everyone to smile._
3. The boy wants the spider _to go away._
4. The kids would prefer the water _to be warmer._
5. The instructor expects the girl _to take her garbage with her._

20 Put in the correct form of the verbs: infinitive or gerund (→ PB p. 76; Grammar → PB G15)

1. "Sorry, I didn't mean _to burn_ (burn) the fish." – "I know, but you should try _to concentrate_ (concentrate) when you're cooking!" 2. "The guy I was with today never stopped _talking_ (talk) about himself." – "Well, remember _to ask_ (ask) if you can have a different partner tomorrow." 3. "I'm sure you'll never forget _meeting_ (meet) that bear!" – "You're right! I'll go on _having_ (have) bad dreams about it for years!" 4. "Have you ever stopped _to think_ (think) where this river comes from?" – "Finding out where it starts would mean _climbing_ (climb) high up into the mountains."

21 Explain what information you need

You are phoning an outdoor adventure center in Colorado.
Turn the questions into infinitive constructions.

TIP Explaining what you want to know often sounds more polite than asking questions.

1. How can I book a course? → I'm calling to find out _how to book a course._
2. Should I do the easy course? → I need advice about _whether to do the easy course._
3. What clothes should I bring? → It would help if you could suggest _what clothes to bring._
4. How do I get to the center? → I'm not exactly sure _how to get to the center._
5. Should I fly to Denver or Aspen? → I don't know _whether to fly to Denver or Aspen._
6. When do I have to pay for the course? → I'd like to know _when to pay for the course._

Unit 3 Seite 41

Check-out 3

26 Change from active to passive (→ PB p. 61; Grammar → PB G11, 12)

1. People are thinking about Route 66 in a whole new way.
   Route 66 is being thought about in a whole new way.
2. They took Route 66 off the maps in 1985.
   Route 66 was taken off the maps in 1985.
3. People have called it the 'Mother Road'.
   It has been called the 'Mother Road'.
4. They are planning a Route 66 car show in California.
   A Route 66 car show is being planned in California.

27 A student's report (→ PB p. 61) (Lösungsvorschlag)

Read a student's report about Zion National Park.
There are things in the report which could be
improved. Underline them and write down what
should be changed.

I think it is amazing that snow and ice made the
landscape of Zion National Park. Over millions
of years the Virgin River carved out Zion Canyon.
5 The really cool pictures that you can see in some
of the rocks were carved out or painted by the
Indians.
In 1917 the first lodge was built and two years
later – I think – Zion National Park was founded.
More visitors visit this national park than any
10 other national park in Utah. In 1930 people

completed the Zion-Mt. Carmel² Highway, which
is 14 miles long.
They offer hikes at the park and that is a good
thing because I like hikes.

Line 1	:	_do not give your own opinion, use the passive_
Line 3	:	_use the passive_
Line 4	:	_do not give your own opinion_
Line 8	:	_only write facts you are sure about_
Line 10 / 11	:	_use the passive_
Line 13	:	_use the passive_
Line 14	:	_do not give your own opinion_

¹Zion [ˈzaɪən] • ²Carmel [ˈkɑːrmel]

Unit 5 Seite 68

28 Relative clauses: The Golden Gate Bridge (→ PB p. 98, Grammar → PB G16)

Turn two sentences into one. (Lösungsvorschlag)
Use relative clauses.

1. The Golden Gate Bridge is one of the sights of San Francisco. It was opened in 1937.
   The Golden Gate Bridge, which was opened in 1937, is one of the sights of San Francisco.

2. Every year millions of people admire the fantastic view. They sometimes cross the bridge more than once.
   Every year millions of people, who sometimes cross the bridge more than once, admire the fantastic view.

3. But fog can be a problem for drivers. It often comes in from the ocean.
   But fog, which often comes in from the ocean, can be a problem for drivers.

4. However, for tourists the bridge can look great even in bad weather. The tourists take photos.
   However, for tourists who take photos the bridge can look great even in bad weather.

29 How to: Show strong feelings (→ PB p. 98) (Lösungsvorschlag)

What can you say to someone who …

1. … keeps pushing a small boy who is waiting for the bus? – *Leave him alone! / Stop it!*
2. … almost crashes into you on his/her bike? – *Hey! Watch out!*
3. … takes your glass and drinks out of it? – *Hey, that's my glass.*
4. … keeps interrupting your conversation with a friend? – *Leave us alone!*

30 Participles: Death Valley today (→ PB p. 98, Grammar → PB G17)

Underline the correct participle.

A (breaking • **growing** • losing) number of tourists is finding out that Death Valley is a(n) (interested • **exciting** • frightened) place to visit. (**Hidden** • Interesting • Experienced) campers and walkers can discover many (**surprising** • hiding • surprised) attractions in the desert. You must wear good walking shoes, but hot feet are better than a (saved • growing • **broken**) leg! If you are (**interested** • surprising • exciting) in history, you could visit one of the (hiding • **surviving** • losing) ghost towns. Tourists don't have to be (frightening • **frightened** • experienced) of Death Valley anymore – but they shouldn't forget those life (-opening • **-saving** • -hidden) water bottles!

Unit 5 Seite 69

31 The right register (Lösungsvorschlag)

Jake would like to have this job. He is talking to Mr. Lopez at the hotel, but he is using the wrong register. Rewrite his role using the polite register.

El Dorado Hotel
We are looking for a friendly teenager 16–18 to welcome¹ guests.
Interested?
Talk to Dave Lopez.

Dave Lopez	Jake
Good afternoon. What can I do for you?	Hi! Where's Dave? *Good afternoon. I'd like to speak to Mr. Lopez, please.*
I'm Dave Lopez. How can I help you?	What about that job in your hotel here? I'm your man! *I'm very interested in the job in your hotel.*
Could you tell me something about yourself and your qualifications?	Sure. Well, I'm a relaxed kind of guy – good with people, friendly. You know the type. I guess. *Yes, of course. I think I'm a friendly person, and enjoy meeting people and helping them.*
We're looking for someone who speaks Spanish and French.	French? Oh no! But my Spanish is – fenomenal. *I don't speak French. I'm sorry, but my Spanish is good.*
Could I ask you to fill in this information, please?	Sure. Give me that pen, will you? *Yes, of course. Could I borrow a pen, please?*

¹to welcome ['welkəm] = empfangen

32 Your US quiz (→ PB p. 99)

a) *Write down the answers.*

1. How many boroughs are there in New York? — *Five*
2. What color are New York cabs? — *Yellow*
3. What game do the New York Yankees play? — *Baseball*
4. What state is the Grand Canyon in? — *Arizona*
5. Which is the highest mountain in the US? — *Mt McKinley*
6. Where did Route 66 start in the east? — *Chicago*
7. What can you see from the Skywalk? — *The Grand Canyon*
8. Which state has the most national parks? — *Alaska*
9. What does every film star hope to win? — *An Oscar*
10. What hit San Francisco in 1906? — *An earthquake*
11. What is the AE word for 'rubbish'? — *Trash*
12. What is the AE word for 'queue'? — *Line*

b) *Write down the last letter of each answer.* e, w, l, a, y, o, n, a, r, e, h, e
Then use the letters to fill in the spaces below:

You have found out a lot about this during the school year:
T H E   A M E R I C A N   W A Y   O F   L I F E

Free Section

Questions

1. What is the name of New York City's famous park?
2. Oh no! Too much traffic in the city.
   Lose a turn.
3. True or false: On September 11, 2001, terrorists
   attacked the Empire State Building.
4. Say one word which you spell differently in British
   and American English.
5. What is the American word for "Gefängnis"?
   (Bonus: Say the British word, too, and go ahead
   2 extra spaces.)
6. Say the name of an Indian tribe.
7. What is another name for "Indians"?
8. You hear a tourist say the word "car".
   You can hear the **r** sound. Is she from Great Britain
   or the US?
9. Open highway! Roll again.
10. Your car does not work.
    Go back 5 spaces.
11. What is the American English word for British
    English "underground / tube"?
12. You fall off your horse at the rodeo.
    Go back 1 space.
13. You win a lot of money at the casino!
    Go ahead 3 spaces.
14. Which word does not belong here?

    hiking   cooking   climbing   cycling

15. Which place is not part of the American West?

    Montana   Arizona   Florida   Colorado

16. You find gold in Alaska!
    Go ahead 2 spaces.
17. A bear steals your food while you are camping.
    Go back 1 space.
18. Which place in southern California is famous for
    surfing: Hollywood, Malibu, or Death Valley?
19. Say the name of the US's neighbors in the South
    and in the North.
20. You fall off your surfboard.
    Go back 7 spaces.

Answers

1. Central Park
3. False.
   They attacked the World Trade Center.
4. e. g. BE / AE: programme / program,
   centre / center, neighbour / neighbor;
   other answers possible
5. jail (AE), prison (BE)
6. Hualapai, Quinault, Shoshone, Navajo, Kaw;
   other answers possible
7. Native Americans
8. She is from the US.
11. subway
14. cooking (not an outdoor activity)
15. Florida
18. Malibu
19. Mexico and Canada

Bildquellen

Umschlag 1 Mauritius (StockImage), Mittenwald; **Umschlag 4** Corbis (Reuters/ Lucy Nicholson), Düsseldorf; **4.1** Avenue Images GmbH (image 100), Hamburg; **4.2** Corbis (Najlah Feanny), Düsseldorf; **4.3** iStockphoto (RF/Tilston), Calgary, Alberta; **4.4** JupiterImages photos.com (RF/photos.com), Tucson, AZ; **6.1** Fotolia LLC (Galina Barskaya), New York; **7.1** Corbis, Düsseldorf; **7.2** Getty Images RF (Photo Disc), München; **7.3** iStockphoto (RF/Tilston), Calgary, Alberta; **7.4** Ullstein Bild GmbH (imagebroker.net/ Jochen Tack), Berlin; **7.5** laif (The NewYorkTimes/Redux), Köln; **7.6** VISUM Foto GmbH (Alfred Buellesbach), Hamburg; **9.1** Alamy Images RM (Black Star), Abingdon, Oxon; **9.2** MEV Verlag GmbH, Augsburg; **10.1** Alamy Images RM (Peter Barritt), Abingdon, Oxon; **10.2** Corbis (Bettmann), Düsseldorf; **11.1** Alamy Images RM (David Ball), Abingdon, Oxon; **11.2** MEV Verlag GmbH, Augsburg; **12.1** Klett-Archiv (Studio Leupold), Stuttgart; **12.2** Mauritius (age fotostock), Mittenwald; **15.1** Picture-Alliance (AFP/George Frey), Frankfurt; **15.2** Reinhard-Tierfoto, Heiligkreuzsteinach; **15.3** Corbis (Torleif Svensson), Düsseldorf; **15.4** iStockphoto (roxana gabor), Calgary, Alberta; **16.1** Avenue Images GmbH (Banana Stock), Hamburg; **18.1** Corel Corporation Deutschland, Unterschleissheim; **19.1** Alamy Images RF (RF), Abingdon, Oxon; **19.2** Alamy Images RM (Janine Wiedel Photolib.), Abingdon, Oxon; **19.3** Alamy Images RM (Black Star), Abingdon, Oxon; **19.4** JupiterImages photos.com (RF/photos.com), Tucson, AZ; **20.1** Avenue Images GmbH (Digital Vision), Hamburg; **20.2** Corbis (Mark Peterson), Düsseldorf; **20.3** Fotosearch Stock Photography (Stockbyte), Waukesha, WI; **22.1** Fotosearch Stock Photography (Stockbyte), Waukesha, WI; **24.1** Avenue Images GmbH (Digital Vision), Hamburg; **24.2** Klett-Archiv (wpunktw, Leipzig), Stuttgart; **25.1** Image 100, Berlin; **27.1** iStockphoto (Claudia Dewald), Calgary, Alberta; **27.2** iStockphoto (Lya Cattel), Calgary, Alberta; **27.3** shutterstock (Stephen Finn), New York, NY; **27.4** iStockphoto (Erik de Graaf), Calgary, Alberta; **27.5** iStockphoto, Calgary, Alberta; **29.1** Avenue Images GmbH (Corbis RF), Hamburg; **30.1** Wikimedia Foundation Inc. (NPS/Public Domain), St. Petersburg FL; **30.2** Mauritius (Kaiser), Mittenwald; **32.1** Corel Corporation Deutschland, Unterschleissheim; **34.1** Fotosearch Stock Photography, Waukesha, WI; **35.1** Corbis (Bettmann), Düsseldorf; **36.1** Getty Images (ABDELHAK SENNA), München; **36.2** shutterstock (Jason Maehl), New York, NY; **39.1** Corbis (Ronnie Kaufman), Düsseldorf; **41.1** Picture-Alliance (Chad Ehle), Frankfurt; **42.1** Global Pictures GmbH (Defd), München; **44.1** Corbis, Düsseldorf; **45.1** Getty Images (David McNew), München; **46.1** Picture-Alliance (epa Randa), Frankfurt; **48.1** Cinetext GmbH, Frankfurt; **49.1** Ullstein Bild GmbH (Lambert), Berlin; **51.1** Bananastock RF, Watlington/ Oxon; **54.1** Picture-Alliance (OKAPIA/Robert Maier), Frankfurt; **55.1** Fotosearch Stock Photography (RF), Waukesha, WI; **55.2** Corbis (Ted Soqui), Düsseldorf; **56.1** Cinetext GmbH (Allstar/Universal), Frankfurt; **56.2** The Moviestore Collection, London; **57.1** kpa photo archive, Köln; **57.1** Corbis (Rune Hellestad), Düsseldorf; **60.1** Corbis (Josef Scaylea), Düsseldorf; **61.1** Das Fotoarchiv (RF), Essen; **62.1** Action Press GmbH (MOST WANTED PICTURES), Hamburg; **63.1** Corel Corporation Deutschland, Unterschleissheim; **64.1** Süddeutsche Zeitung Photo, München; **66.1** laif (Redux), Köln; **66.2** Alamy Images RM (Bill Brooks), Abingdon, Oxon; **66.3** Imago Stock & People, Berlin; **66.4** AKG, Berlin; **68.1** GOODSHOOT (Goodshoot), Annecy-Le-Vieux; **68.2** shutterstock (RF/PSHAW-PHOTO), New York, NY; **72.1** laif (The NewYorkTimes/Redux), Köln; **78.1** iStockphoto (Neta Degany), Calgary, Alberta; **79.1**; **79.2** Ullstein Bild GmbH (Imagebroker.net), Berlin; **79.3** Klett-Archiv (KD Busch Fotostudio GmbH), Stuttgart

Textquellen:
S. 57, ex. 2: © by Percy Adlon, www.percyadlon.com; S.16/17 © by Phil Lamarche. Reproduced by permission of Hodder and Stoughton Ltd.; S.32, ex. 8: © by Jason Williams – Jackson Hole Wildlife Safaris; S.42/43: © by Rosemary Hellyer-Jones; S.72/73: Excerped from the Book La Linea by Ann Jaramillo. © 2006 by Ann Jaramillo. Reprinted by arrangement with Roaring Brook Press, a division of Holtzbrinck Publishing Holdings Ltd. Partnership

Green Line 4

Inhaltsverzeichnis der CDs zum Hörverstehen
Hörverstehenstexte aus Workbook und Schülerbuch

CD 1

Track	Workbook page	Pupil's book page	Exercise	Title / Text	Time
1	4		2	Tips for tourists	04:32
2-3	8		12	Listen for the feeling the voice expresses	01:44
4	10		20	The General Slocum	03:08
5	11		21	Listen to American and British accents	00:52
6	11		23	Listen for keywords	01:24
7-10		22		Chocolate	07:27
11--14	16			American Youth	07:05
15	18		2	A really American game	02:23
16-19		32		The Growl	05:47
20		32	3	Are there differences?	01:12
21-23		34		The fall dance	05:59
24		35	5	Who was it?	02:51
25	30		3	Why are they in Jackson?	04:58
26	31		6	Getting to Jackson	01:35

Gesamtspielzeit: 51'13"

CD 2

Track	Workbook page	Pupil's book page	Exercise	Title / Text	Time
1-5		55		Boy meets girl	13:23
6	39		20	BE or AE?	00:52
7-10	42			The ransom	09:39
11	45		2	I was there – at Wounded Knee	02:39
12-14		66		Between a rock and a hard place	06:20
15		67	4	Looking for danger	03:00
16-18		68		Downriver	06:33
19		69	3	Discussing the story	02:43
20	55		2	Bungee jumping	02:31
21	57		2	A film director speaks	01:59
22	58		2	What do Californians think?	05:09
23-25	63		14	How to: Show strong feelings	02:56
26-28		92		Happily ever after: The Drew Barrymore story	06:43
29-32	72			La línea	07:11
33	76		1	Pronunciation of words	00:47
34-36	76		2	Phrases and sentences	01:32

Gesamtspielzeit: 74'14"